Flora Roy (1912-2008) was a professor at Wilfrid Laurier University in Waterloo, Ontario from 1948 until 1993. Roy received her BA and MA from the University of Saskatchewan and her PhD from the University of Toronto. In 1948 she became a professor in the English Department at Waterloo College (now Wilfrid Laurier University), and served as Department Chair for 30 years. Roy retired from full time teaching in 1978 but continued to teach on a part-time basis until 1993. She received the Confederation Medal in 1967, Queen Elizabeth II Jubilee Medal in 1978, Wilfrid Laurier University Language Arts Award in 1984, and the Wilfrid Laurier University Alumni Association Distinguished Educator award in 1995. In 1988 Flora Roy received an honorary degree from Wilfrid Laurier University.

Jerry Young '64, former student of Dr. Roy, is providing copies of this book to English Majors in 4th-year seminars.

Recollections of
Waterloo College

Waterloo College, Willison Hall, late 1950s.

Recollections of
Waterloo College

Flora Roy

Wilfrid Laurier University Press

WLU

We acknowledge the financial support and services in kind of the Alumni Association, Bookstore, Development Office, Special Initiatives Funding, and University Advancement of Wilfrid Laurier University. We acknowledge the financial support of the Government of Canada through the Book Publishing Industry Development Program for our publishing activities.

Library and Archives Canada Cataloguing in Publication

Roy, Flora
    Recollections of Waterloo College / Flora Roy

ISBN 0-88920-473-X

1. Roy, Flora. 2. Waterloo College—History. 3. College teachers—Ontario—Waterloo—Biography. 4. Waterloo College—Faculty—Biography. I. Title.

LE3.W34R69 2004   378.713'45'092   C2004-904387-0

© 2004 Flora Roy

Cover and text design by P.J. Woodland. Photographs of Willison Hall, Waterloo College. Courtesy of Wilfrid Laurier University Archives and Special Collections.

Printed in Canada

Contents

Editor's Preface

When Flora Roy first came to Waterloo College in 1948 to teach English, she assumed it would be a temporary posting until she finished her PhD and moved on to a larger university. The English department at that time consisted of two faculty members—Flora Roy and Jim Clark—who together offered courses on the entire canon of English literature. But when Flora Roy completed her PhD, she chose to remain at the college.

Dr. Roy was a well-loved and respected teacher and chair of the English Department who also contributed to programs such as Fine Arts and Theatre, Communications Studies, and Film Studies. Although she retired from full-time teaching in 1978, she continued to teach on a part-time basis until 1993. An outstanding educator, she was awarded the Confederation Medal in 1967, the Queen Elizabeth II Jubilee Medal in 1978, and the WLU Language Arts Award in 1984. Dr. Roy was made Professor Emeritus in 1978 and received an honorary Doctor of Letters, also from Wilfrid Laurier University, in 1988. In 1995 the WLU Alumni Association honoured her with the Distinguished Educator Award.

In this vivid collection of anecdotes and memories, Flora Roy takes us on her personal and professional journey as the college is transformed into Waterloo Lutheran University and then Wilfrid Laurier University.

The royalties from the sale of this book will be directed towards funding scholarships.

Chronology

1911   The Evangelical Lutheran Seminary of Canada opens.

1914   Facilities for pre-theological education are established, with courses leading to senior matriculation given by Waterloo College School.

1924   Waterloo College of Arts is established. It provides a four-year program of post-secondary education.

1925   The Faculty of Arts, under the name Waterloo College, is affiliated with the University of Western Ontario. The college offers honours degrees in the arts. (In 1927 there were 87 students.)

1960   Affiliation with Western ends with the college's revised charter, which changes the name of the institution to Waterloo Lutheran University.

1973   On November 1, Waterloo Lutheran University becomes Wilfrid Laurier University, with a student enrolment of 2,299.

Prologue

"THE PAST IS FOREIGN COUNTRY: they do things differently there."
The literary critic and novelist L.P. Hartley was not talking about
Waterloo county when he succinctly described the past as a foreign
country, but his words are apt for my own reflections. The past I
describe in the following pages was not only long ago—1948 to 1960—
but for me it was another country, or perhaps I should say "county."
Waterloo County as I first experienced it almost fifty years ago was
strange to me when I came to Waterloo College, and remains strange
in revisitation.

The period pre-dates the international students' revolts, the
counterculture (including the herbal revolution or the naturaliza-
tion of hemp, hash, and the rest), the Beatles, serial killers, geno-
cide—it is impossible to sum up the changes in interests and
attitudes that cut us off from a time when, although life had its
complications, university life had a very different focus than it does
today.

The *Laurier News* notes subjects that would not have been
treated in the college newspaper in 1948: "Initiatory Fantasy and
Rites of Passage Theory," the Doctor of Ministry in Pastoral Coun-
selling and Marriage and Family Studies, *Bioenergy: A Healing Art*,
New Computer Retailer in WLU Bookstore, *Bodied Mindfulness:
Women's Spirits, Bodies and Places*, CD-ROM Network survey, and
"Sexual Freedoms and the New Right."

To read my recollections of Waterloo College is to travel in a
country far from our present home. For anyone who is searching for

history, the journey will probably be a disappointment. What you will find instead is a series of impressions of what it was like to live and work in an unusual corner of Canada almost fifty years ago.

Given the idiosyncrasies of memory, my own reactions, failures, and achievements will dominate the narrative. The reader must remember that I was only one of a dedicated number who were proud to send out graduates equal to those of the continent's major universities, with a few who were even better than that. With universities fighting for their very existence today in 2004, and with corporate sponsors with their own agendas at the doors—or in some cases inside—it may be a good time to recall the landscape of the era of university expansion when all things academic seemed possible.

PART ONE

Arrival in Kitchener-Waterloo

Flora Roy and Jim Clark in front of Willison Hall,
Waterloo College, 1940s.

I

W<small>HEN</small> P<small>ROFESSOR</small> W<small>OODHOUSE</small> (head of English at University College in Toronto) told me he had arranged that I would meet a couple of men from Waterloo College in his office, I was not very interested. I knew that my time at the University of Toronto was coming to an end, and that I would have to move to some other place, but I also knew that Woodhouse had recommended me for a post in British Columbia—and that he generally got what he wanted from English departments out in the wilderness that was not Toronto.

He seemed to view himself as the guardian of English Studies in Canada. Where there was a vacancy or a weakness, he hoped to remedy the deficiency by supplying just the right person from his roster of Toronto graduates. In fact, he determined who went where across the country. Although his students believed in his vision, English heads (in those days they were appointed heads, not chairs) did not always see things his way, and often not at all. His advantage was that qualified academics were scarce. The men (and a few women) who had come out of the armed forces and headed towards the universities to do graduate work would not be ready for posting for years and, for the same reasons, candidates from Britain and the USA were scarce. There was a phenomenal rise in registration as veterans filled undergraduate classes everywhere. You could, if you could find the space, pack a great many veterans into one section of first-year English, but someone had to mark their term work and finals, and because most heads tried to provide at least some opportunities for supervised discussion in smaller groups, the faculty had to be augmented somehow. There was a market for qualified and experienced university teachers.

I had thought I was one of them, having given courses at the University of Toronto for three years with no complaints. There was no praise either—any compliments I received came from a few students. One wondered if they were just apple-polishing, but I was told that copies of my first-year lectures were being sold in a drugstore on Bloor Street, and I had noticed that my second-year class was crowded with students who weren't on my list, having found out from their friends that they would be able to understand my lectures.

Included in the second-year group were a number of music students who reported that they appreciated my explication of what Milton was about in "Lycidas"—they informed me that the poet's project was what composers of music were about too. In proof of that, they invited me to the conservatory where a professor (I think Weinzweig) would explain what he was trying to do in some of his very new music. I enjoyed that.

Here I was, after two years of assistantships and a year of being at the bottom of the list of real faculty in Toronto (still not finished my thesis), looking forward to a pleasant career in British Columbia. I was not unhappy to meet President Lehmann and Dean Schaus from Waterloo College, but I didn't take them seriously. I gathered that their college was associated with the Lutheran Church of which I knew little more than could be gleaned from a brief study of sixteenth-century European history. From their names I could tell that they were not Scandinavian, so they must be connected with the church in Germany somehow. I had a vague idea of the troubles of Germans in Berlin/Kitchener in the First World War but I had no curiosity about them.

The two visitors were young, slim (even skinny), energetic—Schaus had what seemed like extra nervous energy which, in later interviews, showed itself in the quick successive lighting of cigarettes and in a suggestion of muscles constantly alert to move. The president was more steady and controlled.

We had a pleasant conversation. They didn't ask me anything directly about religion, but at one point in our talk I had reason to say that I didn't agree with Luther in everything, which seemed to amuse them. Dr. Lehmann said, "If you could suit the Sisters of St. John, you'll do for us." (My cv showed two years of teaching in a residential school in Regina run by the sisters. I had lived for four years in one of their residences as a student in Toronto too.)

It was some time before I realized that Dr. Lehmann had graduated from the University of Saskatchewan at the same time as I, and that he had probably done his own investigations by phone calls to the campus, and knew all about my academic career. (I received both my MA and BA there.) Also if he had checked through the Lutheran Church in Saskatchewan, using my home address, he could have turned up a Lutheran somewhere not too far from there, and thus ascertained my parents' position in the community, and my personal reputation. I am not saying that he *did* all this, but, as I later learned, it was possible, and in most cases potential employers did find out more about a candidate than what was in the official documents.

I didn't get the post in BC to Woodhouse's obvious chagrin. "They have made a real mistake," he told me. I never followed it up to find out whom they had appointed or why: my mind was full enough of taking leave of Toronto and insuring that my ties with people there would not be permanently broken. For instance, I subscribed to as many concerts and plays as I thought I could get to—because *faute de mieux* I did accept the post in Waterloo.

Woodhouse informed me he was sending Jim Clark as my assistant, and adjured me to keep up standards. "Clark will be a good worker and colleague," he said. That faint praise gave me little hint of how very valuable Jim would prove to be in the English department and in the college as a whole.

I find it hard to believe now that I had no reservation at all about going to Waterloo. I regarded it as a stop-gap that would support me until I finished my thesis and was qualified to go on to a *real* university. I liked meeting new people, especially if they were different from my usual acquaintances, and I had always been accepted cordially into any community I visited, so I looked forward equally if not eagerly to my first independent position—and the headship.

I didn't realize at first that, when Dr. Lehmann cannily had me promoted to full professor, he was making it very difficult for me to move from Waterloo. The peculiar customs of academia in those days prescribed that you didn't move down in the hierarchy if you went to a new institution—to move as a full professor, I would require more status than I was likely to get at a college where, with two people teaching the whole English curriculum, there would not be much time for the research and writing that made a scholarly reputation.

2

ONE OF THE FEW GRADUATE STUDENTS in my first years at Toronto was an intelligent and attractive young woman who was filling the time while she waited for her husband's military discharge by getting a good MA. She was completely at home in the social world of upper-class Toronto and its satellites and was completely unaffected. Now I realize that she must have known the difficulties I would meet in the tightly knit society of a small city in southern Ontario, and that she was trying, very delicately, to help me. Her husband had returned, they were settled in a house by a lake near Peterborough, and she invited me to spend a weekend there. Among the other guests was a quiet, self-possessed woman from Kitchener-Waterloo. If I had cultivated an acquaintance with her it would probably have given me a foothold in the K-W community, and in time I might have been accepted there. But completely unaware of the codes of Ontario society, it never occurred to me that I would need a sponsor. On the prairies, things were different. I cannot say that I ignored my fellow guest, but I made no attempt to establish any connection. I could not even recall her name afterwards, nor am I aware that I met her in Kitchener later. She may in fact have moved in circles far above those I frequented. It was not my friend's fault that I did not become part of K-W society.

I arrived by train in the spring of 1948, still thinking of myself as a Toronto resident. I didn't pay much attention to my surroundings and, to be honest, I had no intention of staying.

My attention was soon taken up by academic concerns. Before the beginning of term each year, the University of Western Ontario had a day set aside for visits from the affiliated colleges to the central campus to set the curriculum in the various disciplines and to consult about common concerns. A fellow student at Toronto had been on the English faculty at Western for a time and she invited me to stay with her for the duration of the conference. She and the cousin with whom she lived regarded it as my last holiday before my real working life was to begin, and so they included a visit to the London fall fair, and enlivened my reports on the conference with witty and slightly scandalous remarks about the Western faculty. (Old Rawhide—Max Ferguson, the broadcaster—had been an undergraduate with my friend, so stories of his antics before class provided entertaining material for conversation.)

Like all other universities at the time, Western was in transition. The rush of veterans into university classes called for expansion, but the veterans also had lived through some dramatic war experiences that had to be acknowledged. And the influx of students from social groups very different from the English or Scots or Irish, Protestant or Roman Catholic population from which Western had drawn its students would sometimes challenge the curriculum— this was long before official multiculturalism. (WASP was never a very accurate acronym for Canadian governing classes.) It was going to be difficult to meet the needs of the new varieties of students while still maintaining what were called standards, which meant still turning out students who would be acceptable in our governing circles.

The main university had enough to worry about without its affiliated colleges, not all of which were believed to be up to it. Western had complete responsibility for what was taught and for examinations, but in practice the colleges shared in the conferences that set tests and prepared examination papers. Honours papers were graded by UWO professors and general papers *might* be, though I never heard of an occasion for that. Some leeway was allowed in texts: Assumption College in Windsor, which was Roman Catholic, had rather more Chesterton on its syllabus than did Waterloo or Western itself. The sisters at Brescia too had special concerns: when student loans were introduced, the sisters objected to the idea of a "negative dowry" for young women. Usually they were quite aware of what went on in the world (as befitted clever and well-trained Ursulines), and could take care of themselves, but I was told by one of them later that they had appreciated the way our Dean Schaus had always championed them at senate meetings or in university conferences.

There was some concern about guarding the secretary of examinations, and there were rumours of professors who returned from exam conferences to spend the rest of the year teaching only what was on the final paper. And there was the story of the man who kept his promise not to tell his students the questions, but who copied the whole paper on his blackboard and left his students to draw their own conclusions. Experienced markers could spot answers that seemed too much alike to be spontaneous, and discreet questions would be asked of the dean of the college concerned. In those days before active faculty associations or faculty unions, contracts were made and unmade without fuss or publicity.

It all seemed to work quite well but obviously it could not last. Though the time from 1948 when I joined the Western family to about 1957–58 seems now like a golden age, we knew even then that the post-war world would require academic organizations very different from those that had served old Ontario well enough.

3

I HAD NO IDEA THAT I WAS GOING to face so many surprises, some of them not at all pleasant. I was far too sure of myself because of my experience in Saskatoon, Regina, and Toronto where I fitted perfectly in the groups to which I belonged—academic, social, religious, ethnic, even sartorial. I don't think I was arrogant, but I was, as the old people would have said, "at ease in Zion," which was just as likely to annoy people who would have preferred someone with a tentative approach, an outsider hoping to be admitted to a superior and carefully guarded world.

My first visit to my new home was very pleasant. Dean Schaus met me and took me to his home where I had a meal with the family. While last-minute preparation for the meal went on, the young son, about seven or eight years old I think, entertained me. "Would you like to hear a record of my mother's singing?" he asked. Of course I would, like a good guest, but I expected the worst. The first notes of the recorded song surprised me: here was a first-rate voice, professionally trained, sensitive to mood and meaning. I never heard the complete story of the voice, but did learn that when growing up across the American border, the dean's wife had been educated at a Marymount convent. Now here she was, the wife of a Lutheran pastor. She was also strikingly good-looking. Why had she not made a career with her voice, if not in an opera house or recital hall, then in show business?

Settled at the table, we were quiet while the children recited what I gathered was an old German grace: *Jesu Christ, be thou our guest*...and we proceeded to enjoy the meal. (The lady of the house could cook too.) When I left, the son pressed flowers into my hand, and I was sure that all would be well for me in Waterloo. Except that I don't think I was ever seated at that table again.

On my second visit to Waterloo when I came to find some place to live, I stayed overnight in the only possible hotel and was invited on my room's telephone to come down to the bar and meet the caller. The voice was still sober and not at all alarming, but I put a chair-back under the door handle of my room that night, a trick I had learned in the Saskatchewan hinterland. It didn't bother me to learn that k-w had an underside to the family values I saw on my first visit. However, I might have been a little more concerned if I could have known that in the near future, shortly after I moved to Water-loo, a young woman who allowed herself to be picked up in a fairly

respectable coffee bar would be found dead in a field with her stock-
ing knotted around her neck. By that time I was reading the paper
every night hoping thus to make myself at home, and I couldn't see
that there was a great anxiety to solve the crime. The man who
picked her up was soon found, but had an alibi that suggested he
would not have been able to take the body to the field and get back
in the time unaccounted for. The chief of police made a great show
of driving from one location to the other at a furious rate to prove
the point and, as far as I could tell, the case was dropped.

I had heard stories about a violent side to rural and small-town
Ontario in the old days, and though I did not expect to meet the
Black Donnellys in Waterloo, I reminded myself that the God-fear-
ing environment my new landlady was telling me about, had, perhaps, another, less proper aspect.

My landlady! I had not expected to have any trouble finding a
place to live. In those days, cities had women's clubs or residences
where one could stay for a time—or for as long as one wished. They
were comfortable, safe, and companionable. The best known were
the YWCA houses, but there were others. However, in Kitchener and
Waterloo, no one wanted to lodge a young woman—except my landlady. Later I realized I had been set up. One of the seminarians who
had been a friend of her son was anxious that she not be left alone,
and who better to keep her company than a teacher at the college
who would have a lot of time to chat, and especially to listen. I
sensed danger and insisted on looking elsewhere. The slightly embar-
rassed dean took me to the Y, but a shake of the head there meant
no luck. I suspect it was only for the lower classes—girls from farms,
etc., who would work in the rubber factories, perhaps. (I was quite
unaware of the subtle class division in Kitchener-Waterloo.) An
apartment? There was no such thing. An unmarried woman was
expected to live with someone who could be a sort of chaperone. I
eventually resigned myself to the custody of my landlady.

Her husband had been the head of a rubber-manufacturing company in another city, where she had lived with servants (even a chauffeur), and wore perfect clothes to the places where the upper class
drank tea, chatted, and evaluated each other's appearance and stand-

ing. The husband had died suddenly, leaving, I guessed, not as much capital as he would have wished, and the widow returned to her home town with her sons. One was killed in an air force training accident. The other had a promising position with a firm in the USA, and a wife who made it clear that a mother-in-law had no place in her plans for a good marriage. No wonder the seminarian was worried. The poor lady was close to despair, but was hanging on with a pathetic determination not to let her side down. Having a companion (me) would help with the finances—and reassure her about her position in the world. It will not add much to this story of Kitchener and Waterloo to give details of the way I failed her, but one example may be useful.

She wanted to share my literary interests and asked me if I could lend her a book we would study at the college. I thought something Victorian would be safe and lent her George Eliot's *Adam Bede*. In a few days she summoned me to a little talk. "That book—it's all right for me to read it, but my friend, Mrs. X, would be very upset if she thought her girls would read anything like that." I had forgotten that people once believed that young girls should not be informed that an unmarried young woman could become pregnant. But here we were nearly one hundred years after the novel was written, in a Canadian city where obviously some of the citizens still felt that way. Fortunately, there was no biography of the author in the book so my landlady didn't have to grapple with the fact that at her Lutheran college they read books by a woman who lived with another woman's husband.

This incident alerted me to the pitfalls awaiting the English department. It was quite possible that we could have a scandal about requiring students to study immoral works; a concerned parent could have gone to the pastor, and the pastor to the board, but luckily Jim Clark and I never had any real problem about texts.

There were questions, though. The son of a Mennonite bishop was taking my course in American literature. His father picked up the text and, leafing through, discovered that we read Walt Whitman. I don't think he specified his objections—the latent homosexuality, the heresies?—but he expressed his disapproval of our using the work as a set text.

We had a real crisis when Jim Clark produced *The Importance of Being Earnest*. A prominent layman wrote a letter to the Kitchener-Waterloo *Record* pointing out that the play made a mockery of baptism. (The family owning and running the *Record* at that time was Roman Catholic, and not averse to embarrassing Lutherans.) One of the professors at the Lutheran seminary defended us in a letter which declared that the play was a satire on baptisms into Christianity that were numerous at the time. He was thinking of Germany, I suspect, but the situation was not unknown in England. Fortunately, we didn't have any follow-up discussion about conversion, neither the pros and cons nor motives. (And no one at that time objected to our reading of T.S. Eliot in class.)

There were plenty of people in the Twin Cities who lived comfortably with literature from every period, and in several languages, but the world of Waterloo College supporters was divided from them to a degree. There were denominational differences. Most people went to church and a great many made their church the centre of their social life. The university-educated people in town would probably have gone to Victoria College in Toronto which, although it had become United Church, still kept its Methodist flavour, and such people were not interested in a small Lutheran place. Also there was still some lingering memory of the troubles of World War I that kept German and other Lutherans a little apart from the rest of the community. By additional bad luck I was also cut off from the community by a simple fact that Dean Schaus told me many months after I had arrived on campus. His explanation cleared up my situation though it did not make it any easier.

The elite of Kitchener and Waterloo had decided that the vacancy in the English department at the college should be filled by one of their own. It does not matter now who she was. I think she would have been quite acceptable except that she would probably never have gone on to the PhD, and Dr. Lehmann was looking for candidates who would help to build the college up to genuine university status—though I do not know if he ever hoped for an independent university. Instead, the position had gone to an outsider, and no one, except perhaps Dr. Lehmann, was very pleased.

Although I did not know the reason, I sensed the displeasure of the choicer spirits of the Twin Cities when I accepted the almost mandatory invitation to the year's first meeting of the University Women's Club. I was told that someone would give me a lift to the meeting, and along came several ladies—one of them the woman who had wanted my job. If I had known that, I would have appreciated the nobility of her seeming to sponsor me as a member of what was, in those days, an exclusive body. There were not many female university graduates then, but those few regarded themselves as the guardians of culture and learning.

I had been a member of the University Women's Club in Regina and had enjoyed the discussions at the meetings where everyone was relaxed and most people were entertaining. However, here was a stiffness of people come together for a good cause, doing their duty with no extra camaraderie. For the first time in my life I drank my coffee alone in a gathering; no one came to talk to me. On the way home, two of the women in the car chatted about the hospital board—also, it appeared, a place only for those who belonged. "That woman from Saskatchewan," said one of them, "how did *she* get on the board?" I realized that there was more than one area marked "No trespassing by outsiders." Today, after all the changes wrought by the development of two universities, and all the shifts in status caused by the departure of old industries to the south, the state of local society I have described in these examples seems to have been a bad dream, but it was real enough. There must have been easygoing, amusing people about, but those I met mostly seemed to be constrained about behaving properly, and doing their duty by supporting worthy organizations. Pub culture was not common: jollity, when it came, was heavy-footed and loud.

4

I WAS SOON TO KNOW THAT THERE was more than a lingering memory of the "troubles" that had occurred in Berlin/Kitchener during the First World War. But, before I recount my personal experiences,

I want to call on what I have learned about the community since 1948, rather than following the story of my own gradual understanding. That means tackling two topics which, in the past, no polite person would have raised in a general gathering in the Twin Cities. The second was what might be called "denominationalism"; for the first I have no name. "Racism" will not work, for people of the same ethnic background, even members of the same family, were on opposite sides in the dispute. Let us call it "*them* and *us*-ism." "We" were (and are) those who wanted the British, French, and Russian forces to win the war and "they" had an equal partiality for Austria-Hungary and Germany, not to mention Turkey, and, at first, Italy.

Today the Berlin/Kitchener affair looks to most like a tempest in a beer mug. There is some belief that "we" were quite irrational and prejudiced in objecting to the expressed hopes of "them," and there may even be some sympathy today for those who were opposed to British imperialism. At the time there must have been people who felt that it *would* matter if their favoured imperialism could win. A German victory would probably have left Britain much as she is today, but her colonies, dependencies, and spheres of influence would most likely have come under German hegemony. Playing the game of "what if?" further, one can conjecture that a victorious Germany might have made an alliance with the USA (which had reason at the time for resenting Britain) and that Canada might have become a joint German/American sphere of influence.

There were also more personal reasons for preferring one side or the other. "We" had sons, brothers, and husbands fighting the male relatives of the other side; the enthusiastic partisanship aroused at an old-fashioned hockey game must have been much magnified when the opponents were dying by thousands in a real war. Not to labour the point, the outcome of the war mattered, and it is no wonder it was taken seriously. What is more pertinent to my personal story and Waterloo College is that the community remained divided by deeply felt animosities that lasted, as I discovered, into and beyond the Second World War.

When the battle of the universities was taking place, I once discussed the Berlin/Kitchener affair with a colleague who had come from an Irish community near London. The two of us—strangers in Waterloo County—confessed our inability to understand the intensity of emotion engendered by the dispute, and each mentioned that it must have something to do with the First World War, though we were not sure what.

Several years after the final break between the universities, a newcomer to the community told me that when she had inquired about the existence of two such institutions she was told, "It was all the fault of the Germans." This seems a good example of blaming the other (that is, *them*), and testifies that over fifty years after the battle of Berlin/Kitchener "the other" was still vaguely German.

I have not read any studies of Waterloo County during the Second World War, but I have been assured by a friend that it was very uncomfortable to grow up here as a member of a German-speaking family. On the other hand I have also been told that there was a good deal of sympathy here for the Third Reich. One woman described how a visitor to her home once expressed forcefully his adherence to Hitler's cause, ignoring the prominently placed pictures of the family's sons in Canadian uniform. "He was never invited back," said my friend. Someone else told me of a gathering where German women made merry, laughing at Canadian uniforms, especially the boots. (They were not alone in their opinion. I have heard that Canadian soldiers sometimes helped themselves to German boots when the wearers had no further need for them.)

I have never heard anything of a stand taken by Waterloo College in the original confrontation between supporters of Britain and those of Germany. The college authorities seem to have kept out of the dispute, which would not have endeared them to either side. For the period of the Second World War, I do have information about Nazi activities on the college campus. One of the faculty members had a large swastika banner in his office, and during a summer school there was a young instructor who was assumed to be trying to recruit supporters for the Nazi cause. Apparently he was doing a little blackmailing on the side, telling Germans in the area that he would denounce their relatives in Germany to the Gestapo if he was not paid to desist, and the German authorities found him out and quietly removed him. At any rate, whether the Mounties or the Gestapo got him, he just disappeared and nothing was ever heard of him again. The swastika banner disappeared too.

I can believe that there was attempted recruitment of supporters for Hitler here, because I had come across it in Saskatchewan. Agents had travelled from one German community to another there just before the war, and after their visits pictures of Hitler appeared in German homes. A fellow student at university told me he was employed by the Mounties to infiltrate a "bund" that had been formed about twenty-five miles from where I grew up. He was rather amused by the meetings he attended where the order of business was heavy drinking, so that afterwards members could be found recumbent along the paths that led to their nearby homes. At the time we didn't take them seriously, but at the outbreak of war, there were numbers of Germans picked up by the police and held until it could be determined if they were dangerous.

The precautions might seem excessive today, but at the time the great fear was of sabotage. Even in Saskatchewan, explosives detonated under a culvert when a troop train was going over could have done a lot of damage. (Everyone had access to dynamite and caps, especially for well-drilling.) How much more vulnerable were the factories in the k-w area that produced materials of war! One can understand, while deploring, the suspicions people may have had of their German neighbours. And even if Waterloo College had cleansed itself in time of its Nazi symbols, there may have remained some distrust of the college in the community.

I can illustrate the division in the community with two personal experiences, one of which occurred very shortly after my settling in the community, the other sometime later.

Among the new faculty at Waterloo College, I was delighted to meet a young man I had met during the war when I was brushing up my French at a summer school in Banff. He was German, separated from his home and family by the war. He was intelligent, witty, and generally good company. It was good to know that he would be a colleague in this college which seemed to be on the way to becoming an admirable little post-secondary institution. He had made contact with a local German friendship society and was involved in

raising funds for German relief. There was to be some sort of concert in aid of the cause, and I readily agreed to attend. After all, I
did not wish the Germans to starve. I hope the money he raised *did*
make it possible to save some lives, but now I realize how confused
the situation must have been for anyone attempting to be a good
Samaritan in that place and at that time. There were Germans who,
as they told me themselves, had not really suffered during the war.
But as we have since learned, there were also others, mostly prison-
ers-of-war in American hands, who lived in frightful conditions.
The widow of a German colleague told me that her father saw friends
die of cold and hunger in the American zone. I don't think our German relief could have got to them. Her husband, on the other hand,
was quite comfortable as a prisoner of the British. "It may have
helped that his commander and the English commander had been
at Oxford together," she said. Even after the war, one reason for the
continuation of rationing in England in 1950 was apparently that
supplies were being diverted to help feed Germans, who probably
didn't need extra aid from Kitchener and Waterloo. Then there were
the people under the Russians who were almost certainly beyond our
reach, and those who were captured by Canadians. I don't know
what our official records say, but I was told that it was usual to dis-
arm prisoners of the Canadians and say, in effect, "Shoo!" as they
trudged off to look after themselves.

Back in 1948, I didn't give much thought to the realities of life
for Germans, and was quite happy to contribute the price of my concert ticket to their relief.

I told my very new landlady when I was going to a fundraising
event and was amazed by her reaction. "Don't have anything to do
with those people," she commanded, and would say nothing further. In fact she didn't speak to me again for quite some time, putting my breakfast and dinner on the table with a stony face of
condemnation. I don't think her reaction came entirely from blaming the enemy for her son's death in the training flight, and I never
heard her later express revulsion at the information we were grad-
ually accumulating about extermination camps. I think it is reasonable to suppose that her parents had taken the anti-German side in

the First World War and that she was simply keeping up the fight.

My second experience came after I had discussed with a class a new short story I had read which seemed to illustrate the aspects of the genre I wanted to recommend for aspiring writers. It was called "Address Unknown." Written in epistolary form, it told the story of a German Jew, living abroad, who writes to a German who is his sister's lover and his own dear friend. The sister disappears, her sweetheart having done nothing to try to save her. From that time the German receives letters, apparently in code, hinting at Jewish origins for his family. He pleads with his Jewish friend to stop the game, but it continues until the last letter is returned by a still efficient German postal service, stamped "Address Unknown."

Sometime after class a student asked to see me. He was white with distress, and could hardly tell me what was wrong. "That story...it's immoral...cruel." I couldn't believe it. Here was someone talking from the other side of the looking glass. I had to admit that I had shared in the writer's wish to punish the German and had not really regretted his fate. In extenuation I could say that my whole moral grounding had been shaken by the revelations of the "Final Solution" as we learned more and more of the details about what we now call the Holocaust. But I was looking from my side of the mirror. For him there were only the beleaguered Germans protecting themselves as best they could from enemies within and without. I don't recall what I said to him, but I probably talked about structure, compression, and language while I was looking at his innocent face and blond hair, thinking, "There is more here than an ethical problem." Afterward I made discreet inquiries, and, yes, his family had been known German sympathizers in the 1939–45 war. I think of them now, a little bewildered, living among people who saw events from a perspective totally impossible for them to understand. Later when the "split" came, this family supported the University of Waterloo. Was it because they hoped it would make possible a new kind of vision for the community, quite different from views that were pro-this and anti-that?

And how many members of the community had for years gone about their daily lives in the Twin Cities with a surface sociability that hid the painful division, the incomprehension about the feelings and views of the "others"?

5

In my first years in Kitchener-Waterloo, practically everyone belonged to a congregation and worshipped on Saturday or Sunday. I also went off dutifully—and hopefully—to the nearest Anglican church. My landlady was Lutheran, as were many of my colleagues, and in time I met representatives of most of the other religious denominations to be found in Canada. On the surface it appeared that the community lived together in complete harmony, and it would have been impolitic as well as impolite to suggest anything else. Under the surface were common human weaknesses, especially prejudice and competitiveness. I never realized their extent until we were negotiating about the structure of the not-yet-existent University of Waterloo. The story of the Associate Faculty of Waterloo College, which became that university, I want to postpone until later but I can tell at this point one story that made me at last aware of the uneasy relations between some of our local denominations. I was called to the telephone—I recall that I was proctoring an examination in the Seagram Stadium—to be addressed by an official of the parish in which I was enrolled. "I had to tell you," he said in excitement, "I've just come from a meeting about the new university and we are going to be equal to the Lutherans!" This is a fairly literal report of his words. If an Anglican college, starting with nothing, were to be equal to that of the Lutherans, one would have to gain, and the other lose a very great deal. And how long had he been controlling his envy of the Lutherans who owned the college buildings on Albert Street that were a sign of domination in the community? To some they must have seemed a stronghold of Germanism with professors from Germany and the cluster of expatriates who were attracted by something like the culture they had left in the fatherland. To others they were a sign of Lutheranism, of people who professed to be Protestant but would not think of merging into other like groups and losing their slightly foreign identity. And there were probably some who were reminded that the owners of those buildings were reputed "to have all the money."

I never became an expert on Lutheranism, but I did see it change during my years on the campus. In spite of a German presence in the college and seminary, the main influence at the time of my arrival was from the United States. It was quite some time before the Canada Synod became independent. I was invited on one occasion to go to Gettysburg for a sort of convention of colleges related to the church. One of our faculty members, whose grandparents had been living in the environs of the city during the engagement that made it famous, showed us around the battleground. I still recall the scene and the mental pictures I brought back of Pickett's Charge and other events he described. The link of a Lutheran gathering with memories of a famous battle opened up the idea of Lutheranism for me beyond the confines of Waterloo County.

The conference seemed to fix upon the question of whether there should be church-related colleges at all. Finances were a problem even in the country of wealthy donors—and any local assumption that Waterloo Lutherans were unduly rich was not very well founded. I saw that perhaps the days of Waterloo College were numbered, but there were no signs of decline on the campus. Enrolment was rising, there was a new dining room cum lecture hall, a women's residence, and a new teaching building. The community must have been taking notice of the academic success of the Lutherans.

If there was any envy, any distrust of people who were different, it would not have been allayed by the way the Lutheran presence must have appeared to an unsympathetic viewer. I have mentioned the college buildings, but there were also the fine churches, which in those days dominated the cityscape. One in Waterloo burned spectacularly, and its high spire no longer attracted attention, but there were plenty left. As I try to recall those days, I can see the Lutheran clergy, the older ones aware of their prestige in the congregations. One of them always appeared in public dressed as he would have been in old Germany, not with a common clerical collar, but with a front all in white, from hair, moustache, wing collar, bow tie—to, I think, a white vest. The details are dim now, but I do recall that he was an impressive sight. There were deaconesses too, going about their supportive work in the parishes, in grey habit, and grey bonnets with the symbolic veil, set apart from the crowd. Having come from years of association with Anglican nuns who wore the full Benedictine habit, I felt quite comfortable with these slightly exotic forms of life, but I can see that some of the citizens of the Twin Cities may have resented them.

On the campus, I never found the Lutheran connection to be in any way discomfiting. The faculty and the student body were drawn from all shades of skin as well as of opinion, though the president and dean, and the board of governors were Lutheran. There was a service each day in the old chapel in the original red ivy-covered building, with its stained-glass window representing the text, "Behold, I stand at the door, and knock." (Where is it now?) Attendance was voluntary at that time. The Christ or coffee crisis came when we were Waterloo Lutheran University, under President Villaume. Faculty were expected to attend chapel to set a good example. But not all students felt inspired. In fact there seemed to be a conflict between chapel (i.e., Christ) or a coffee break. My most poignant recollection of the religious side of the college is of a chapel service attended by a young woman whose father was near death. Dean Schaus was the officiant. I recall no details of the prayers or the brief sermon, except that we all left the place feeling strengthened for what might come. The student's father recovered.

Later we were to be charged with censorship of teaching on religious grounds, involving vague appeals to the Canadian Association of University Teachers (CAUT) in the name of academic freedom. In my first years on campus there was no obvious control of expression, but when interviewing candidates for faculty positions, I think the administration tried to winnow out those who would be hostile to Christianity.

Lutheranism as represented in the college seemed to be in a period of transition. Some of the older clergy retained an authoritarianism that was resented. I heard complaints from parishioners concerning ministers who dictated what each family should give to the church, and who exerted a fairly strict discipline over the flock. My landlady, for instance, was interested in Swedenborgianism but told me she didn't dare embrace that faith because she wanted to be buried beside her husband and knew that would be impossible if she strayed from the Church.

The younger clergy were being trained in the social sciences as well as in theology—perhaps *more* than in theology—and would bring about marked changes. I believe that the broad pre-theology programme at the University of Western Ontario, as it was taught at Waterloo College, had something to do with producing a new generation of pastors who had more understanding of life in Canada in the second half of the twentieth century than had their predecessors, many of whom trained in Germany for overseas service in a world that had disappeared.[1]

Before I leave this unhappily superficial sketch of Lutheranism and Waterloo College, I must stress the way in which the college was tied to the local and country congregations through the efforts of the Ladies' Auxiliary and the College Boarding Club. The women were foster mothers to the boys in residence, especially the seminarians. I recall especially the quilts they made for the students' beds. The Boarding Club, which was the student group that provided meals for residents, had a friendly raid each fall on the surrounding parishes, returning with provisions for the winter. It is evident that people who may have known little about post-secondary education could feel they had a stake in *their* college through their quilts and vegetables.

On weekends in the spring the faculty went out into parishes all over Southern Ontario where they forged links with the parishioners, speaking to the young people about possible vocations—worldly as well as clerical—and generally making the Lutheran college a part of their lives.

It is not strange to me that when the time came for that institution to be "cut down to size," to be equal only to a group of other

---

1   I do not believe that a thoroughly satisfactory history of German Lutheranism in Canada has been written yet. I have been told that the clergy sent out to Canada were all trained in a certain institution which may have inculcated ideas and procedures in parishes and seminaries whose influence could be seen here practically into the 1960s. I hope someone will undertake such a history as a doctoral thesis, to be done before all memories of those times have been lost.

small denominational residential colleges of the new University of Waterloo, they were not eager to surrender without a fight.

6

I HAVE HEARD FROM A TEACHER IN MACGREGOR SCHOOL nearby that she has in her grade 8 class Croats, Serbs, Christian Kurds, Muslim Kurds, and representatives of most of the other ethnic or religious groups mentioned in the news reports of world unrest that we hear daily. In view of the possibilities for trouble in our contemporary mix of population, it seems almost trivial to note denominational differences in Kitchener-Waterloo just after the Second World War and their effect on our history. However, I do feel that they played some part in the events that led to Waterloo Lutheran splitting away from the University of Waterloo, and thus deserve at least a mention.

Dean Schaus once told me with pride that we had more Roman Catholic students than Lutherans. There was a local college, St. Jerome's, associated with the University of Ottawa, to which they might have gone, but both institutions had less than satisfactory academic reputations at that time, and ours mustn't have seemed too threatening. Although our Catholic students seemed quite comfortable in the midst of Lutheranism, there could have been some prejudice in their elders. It was said that the family who owned the *Record* was not very friendly to Lutherans and, certainly in the months of acrimony as we moved towards the "split" from the new University of Waterloo, their reports of the situation seemed always to put us in an unfavourable light.

I realize that Brother Martin Luther has been pardoned by the Church for his theses, but back in the Kitchener-Waterloo of just after the Second World War, some Roman Catholics may still have resented the rebel. I once asked Dean Schaus, one of the few Lutherans originating in Bavaria, whether it was true that in that part of Germany the word "Luther" was always preceded by the word *Teufel* (Devil Luther). He chuckled and replied, "Yes, and you had to spit after pronouncing it."

The most exotic religious element in the community were the Mennonites. The "Russian" Mennonites were among our best students. They lived inconspicuously in the general world and did not resemble the "old order" Mennonites in any obvious way. When the "split" came, a Mennonite college in Winnipeg became our affiliate for some years, and one of their members became in time our president (Peters). (Conrad Grebel College was a later development.)

The "old order" Mennonites were distinguished generally by their garb and by their horses and buggies. There was an entire mythology among non-Mennonites about the code by which they governed their lives. For example, they were said to paint the front porch blue if there was a marriageable daughter in the house. They didn't have much contact with Waterloo College, but one of their number became an Honours English student and captured academic honours, first with us, then at the Medieval Institute of the University of Toronto, and in the scholarly world of Europe and the USA.

I never saw a breakdown of our student body into the various denominational groups represented there but I think we could have found some of practically every local church or sect. A few stand out in my memory. Among our most loyal defenders at the time of the split were "Continuing Presbyterians," that is, Presbyterians who did not join with Methodists and Congregationalists to form the new United Church of Canada. Their championship of the Lutheran college may have been on personal grounds rather than for historical reasons: a member of one of their leading families had been an enthusiastic graduate of ours—and, like some other people in the Twin Cities, her family had long distrusted the man who became the president of the University of Waterloo.

One religious group that especially interested me was made up of the Swedenborgians. We had several students from that body, and they were among our best-prepared and most able. At that time, anyone interested in English literature knew Northrop Frye's work on Blake's poetry, which in part owed something to Swedenborg. Our students were pleased that I had heard of the New Jerusalem Church, but were not much impressed with Blake. (My landlady too had been delighted to learn that I knew something of Swedenborg, but was dashed to discover that I would not join with her as a disciple.) I had an impression after the "split" that local Swedenborgians at least did not resent the new face of Waterloo College as Waterloo Lutheran University.

The United Church and the Anglicans were the two denominations, after the Roman Catholics, that had most to do with the way in which the new University of Waterloo came to be formed. I say "came to be" because the development was gradual, and not, I think, planned from the beginning.

Our Dr. Herman Overgaard was one of those who persuaded the relevant officials in Ottawa that student residences could become eligible for financial backing under the National Housing Act. Thus Waterloo College, though a church-related institution, could obtain mortgages for the provision of housing for students. As may be expected, other religious denominations were not far behind.

I jokingly refer to myself as the prime mover in the founding of St. Paul's College at the University of Waterloo. I was once entertaining my English Department colleagues from the University of Western Ontario with the latest stories about the jockeying for primacy among religious groups in Kitchener and Waterloo as they grabbed up their share of the newly available mortgage money. I hadn't noticed that one of them wasn't laughing until he pushed back his chair and stood up, saying, "Well, if that's what's going on, we're going to get into it!" I recognized a United Church layman whose father-in-law was the wealthy and generous donor of a women's residence at Western, and I wasn't surprised when I learned that, indeed, the United Church would have a college on the new campus.

I have already mentioned that at least one Anglican was rejoicing that the Lutherans would be cut down to size, and I suspect he was not alone. I was not in any position to hear the opinions of any other church representatives, but it is conceivable that the United Church also wouldn't mind learning that it might become equal to the Lutherans. At the time of the troubles in the First World War, there were those who left the Lutheran Church to join other Protestant denominations that would have less association with Germany in the public mind, and some of those chose Methodism which in time became part of the United Church.

It was probably as a symbolic gesture that President Hagey of the new University of Waterloo broke his own ties with Lutheranism and joined the United Church of Canada once he was sure that the Lutherans of Waterloo College were going their own way in spite of him. His university would represent the mainstream of local society, well-meaning, not too doctrinal, upper middle-class and rising, and comfortable with the corporate ethic of local industry and finance.

The Anglicans in Kitchener and Waterloo had local features too. I had come to the Twin Cities from an Anglo-Catholic environment and had been warned that Huron diocese was different. I was told that one of the nuns I knew had been warned by her confessor not to take communion there. (How important that sort of thing was then! What would he think about the new God Mother/Father service that was tried out at the recent diocesan meetings in Huron?)

My first impressions of the church nearest to my landlady's apartment were not very favourable. The extremely well-meaning rector had some difficulty in holding our attention while the intellectually challenged (then called idiot) son of the caretaker was in a front pew, but sitting half-turned around so that he could make faces at the congregation all through the service. The next rector dealt with that diversion immediately and drastically but I had by then moved to Kitchener, and to St. John's church where the services proceeded with decorum. I even joined the ladies' choir that sang vespers each Sunday, but finally vespers was abolished and we were to join the general choir—and by that time I had moved back to Waterloo. I have kept up my parish membership in St. John's, but at Easter find my way to a more traditional service in Toronto.

I tell all this so that you will know why an official of St. John's telephoned me to give me the good news about becoming equal to the Lutherans. I learned only later that my colleague, Jim Clark (whose wife was a member of the same congregation), was also approached, but more definitely invited to work against the Lutherans. "They want us to turn against the people who pay our salaries," I am told he remarked. In other words, they were claiming *us* as their own, against *them*, the strangers with German names and who knows what unCanadian ideas. The fact that a great many Anglicans had German names too just reminded everyone that they had had the good sense to leave the foreign environment of the Lutheran church in the time of the First World War.

Speaking of foreign names, there was a young Estonian woman named Ilse Aksim, who married a man named Stewart. The local Estonians were distressed to learn that she was marrying a man with such an outlandish name. It's all in your point of view.

7

IT IS TEMPTING TO GO ON WITH IMPRESSIONS of the culture and civilization of the area in and surrounding Kitchener and Waterloo, but topics such as politics and social relationships may perhaps be better postponed until after I have gotten myself on the campus and immersed in the community that would in time become the base for my professional life.

The physical setting was not exactly a shock. After all, I had just come from Toronto where I had worked in a tiny office upstairs in the cloisters, an area that pretended to be medieval, and in some ways succeeded. For instance I recall when at last washrooms were installed in the subterranean area, about 120 years after the building was constructed.

Waterloo College was a red-brick building that combined classrooms, gymnasium, library, and residence rooms for male students—and washrooms which, I remember, could be sensed as one came in the main entrance. There was a dining room where the students' Boarding Club provided meals, based, as I have mentioned before, on donations of food from the parishes.

There were no faculty offices at first, at least not for me. I recall talking to a Ghanian student about his future training in an anteroom to the ladies' washroom—not exactly a salubrious location. I don't recall where I put my outerwear when I changed into the gown that, like all my colleagues, I wore in the lecture rooms. Indeed, I recall that I once deliberately left my coat on the floor outside the office of one of the college officials, remarking that I couldn't find anywhere else to put it. Before long there were hooks installed.

Examinations were held in the gym where the uneven floor could trip the unwary. We followed all the rules for exams that were dictated by Western, including the registration of all those who were writing. The head of Romance Languages pointed out to me on one of those occasions that the difference between the French mentality and ours was that a Frenchman would make his first count of students and then throughout the invigilation period would count again and again, each time getting a different answer. Much later in my life I found out his stereotyping was not completely removed from the facts. A French Canadian nun who had just taken a summer course in France told me with much amusement that when the class went on an excursion in a bus, the French sister in charge counted the passengers repeatedly without coming to a decisive sum. But to return to Waterloo College—in fact to do so you took the trolley bus which went only as far as what is now the corner of King Street and University. You then climbed a few little slopes as you angled past the back of Mrs. Aksim's garden to arrive at the college. Over in the direction of what became University Avenue, there were some low coops where Nick kept his chickens.

Nick! He was the master of the campus: groundsman, cleaner, repairman, furnace man, and much else. When he left us to go to the University of Waterloo it was said he took with him in his head the location of all the underground pipes and wiring that supplied the college buildings, but we did manage to survive without him. Nick came from Central Europe (Romania? Somewhere in the old Austria-Hungarian Empire, no doubt.) People said that he had lived with the gypsies, which may have helped to give him a certain *insouciance*. His rather heavy-set presence of medium height haunted the place. The two women who worked in the library reported skirmishes in which they successfully put book stacks and reading desks between themselves and Nick, but he didn't bother the female faculty, though a former dean of women told me once that every night, when he cleaned, Nick moved her heavy desk to a place that was inconvenient and every morning she moved it back. Nick made use of anything on campus that he needed, including the "boarding" of his collection of exotic fish in a tank in one of the science labs. When the student-engineers of our new associate faculty arrived in our midst, some of them felt a similar freedom. One day they were discovered feeding Nick's fish to a piranha in a neighbouring tank, which seemed to me a *quid pro quo*. I shall give just one more example of Nick's assurance: when it was decided to house the college president off campus, the existing "president's house" on Albert Street became redundant. Nick offered to clear it away, and with the aid of a troop of his buddies, inspired by a number of cases of beer, the demolition was effected—with a great deal of cheerful noise from the roof—and the whole house rebuilt later on a site where Nick chose to make his new home. I have gone on about Nick to try to establish a feeling for the kind of informality that has, since my coming at least, characterized the institution that has become Wilfrid Laurier University.

Today there are numbered parking lots. Then there was just one beside Willison Hall where, on chilly mornings, the students would be pushing the house father's little Austin until it would splutter and start. Willison Hall used to sit in what is now the parking lot between the Seminary and the Woods Building. It was demolished in the late 1960s. By the way, I had to learn the terms house father (hausvater) and house mother (hausmutter) for the heads of the residences. The German connection was sometimes very obvious. There was a residence for young women (girls in those days), an ordinary dwelling house which had been taken over. Later the old house went to the college and the building was remodelled and turned into a real residence with a special clothes closet for the hanging of gowns, *de rigueur* for college balls in those days.

I realize that I have been trying to avoid writing about the academic problem that greeted me when I started my work at Waterloo College, a problem that would have caused me to resign at the end of the year, if not before, if I hadn't been aware of letting Professor Woodhouse down—not to mention all the women who might become heads of English departments if I could pull it off.

The curriculum was clear enough. We had agreed in our preterm conference at Western on how we would approach the texts. I myself would have to do some reviewing but with my experience as student and lecturer, I had no misgivings about my ability to teach the courses. Things seemed to go well in the general arts programme, but in the honours courses the students and I seemed to have diverse aims, and I couldn't elicit any particular enthusiasm from them. I knew I was pushing them hard—the Western English programme in those days was very heavy—but I had no doubts about my own contribution to our common education.

A vague rumour started to reach me of student protests, including a letter from one young man who hoped to graduate at the end of the year, demanding, I think, my immediate dismissal. I never *did* see the letter so I am unsure about details. It may have been sent to the college newspaper, the *Cord*, then shown to the administration and censored before publication. I cannot say that I felt hurt—just certain that somehow I was in the wrong place at the wrong time. I gathered that the president refused to be influenced by the complaints, but my colleagues in other departments were not particularly supportive—just wary. Anyway I carried on to the end of the year. After the examinations were safely passed by all the students (with one exception), then came the convocation celebrations. At one of them the student who had complained sought me out to thank me. "I didn't know what you were doing until I saw the exam paper," he said. I felt justified, but still didn't know why he had been so emphatic in his disapproval. Several years later I heard the story of the problems at the English department of Waterloo College in the year preceding my coming.

There had been one crisis at Western that resulted in their hiring the head of *our* English department at the last minute, leaving the college without a faculty, really. Somehow Waterloo was persuaded to hire an old gentleman, a former head at Western, to fill the gap. Assisting him was a young lady, very attractive, they say, her head full of her coming marriage so that all her spare time was taken up with trips all over Southern Ontario with her mother to gather her trousseau (yes, they had them in those days).

The old gentleman was much loved on our campus, I was often told. He *was* in fact very much a gentleman, bringing flowers to the secretaries, and always had a courteous word for anyone. His classes were very pleasant, just friendly discussions in a warm, intimate atmosphere with no sense of strain. I learned the result of all this much later when some of the faculty at Western were recalling that period. When the examination papers arrived to be marked there, the faculty were at a loss. "We didn't know what to do with them," said one. He didn't tell me what they did, but I guessed that the addition of enough bonus marks would have evened things out, so that the English honours class of Waterloo College graduated with no questions asked. That had been all very well for them, but next year the students I met were sadly disappointed when they realized that the new professor expected carefully researched and written seminar papers, along with a sound knowledge of the texts.

The one exception who did not do well in the examinations was a young woman, very pleasant and friendly, whose father had made a point of picking me up many a morning in his car when he was taking her to school. The head of the Western English department who had the final word in evaluating our honours papers told me he didn't think she should continue in honours; after reviewing her work and her potential I agreed, so she was moved back into general arts. I then left for Saskatchewan and missed the cataclysm that ensued. It seemed that family honour was at stake. A cousin had attained an honours degree, so this poor girl was expected do the same. There were demands and petitions to everyone possibly involved, including the head at Western. It was claimed that I was an ingrate: "And after all the rides we gave her!" said the father. When I repeated his remark to the head at Western he said, "That settles it," and he rejected the petition. The student in question finally went to the USA to get a degree that would satisfy family pride.

The whole affair caused me to wonder about university standards. All through my time as department head, then chair, I was concerned about whether we were meeting academic requirements. We really had no norm except that if our graduates did well in MA courses in other universities, we were probably on the right track. In the UK they have external examiners for students graduating with the first degree. Here generally this has become common for the PhD but it seems to me we could profit from an outside opinion even for the BA. Marking English examinations is a subjective business. While we were affiliated with Western we had to satisfy their examiners, which was a very good apprenticeship, but when we were independent it was difficult to train new, inexperienced faculty to assess the standing of their students. The situation I met in my first year, after only a year of wavering from an appropriate standard in the department, can surely not have been unique. I became skeptical about CVs and even about examination results of candidates for positions if I did not personally know the markers and the conditions in the departments concerned at the time. This was after I discovered a serious discrepancy between paper qualification and performance which I must describe later, and which came from a change in department personnel such as the one at Waterloo College that gave us so much trouble.

By the time another year had passed with our students meeting the approval of the examiners at Western, I was quite firmly established in the college, academically at least.

8

WHEN DEAN SCHAUS TOLD ME that I was not too welcome in the community because another candidate had been favoured for my position, he added, "You will find your friends here," meaning "at the college." I did, in the end, but it took time, several years in fact. I found that there was a perhaps unconscious tendency to favour my assistant, a handsome young man with an attractive personality and an assured air. The secretaries seemed always to consult him about departmental business, instead of me. There was, I think, the feeling that a woman could not make decisions, and it took some time to establish, without being overbearing, the fact that I was in charge. Indeed, not until we became independent did I really have control of the English department.

It must have been difficult for my assistant, Jim Clark, who throughout was exemplary in his attitude to me. I was, however, very pleased when he became the major commanding the campus COTC (Canadian Officers' Training Course, i.e., campus cadets) because he then didn't have to be second in command in all his campus activities. Later when we were independent he became a first-rate head of our Extension Services, but more of that later. So the faculty and staff in general accepted me slowly. I had to change, as did they.

As I look back, trying to see why I might have alienated at first the people who later would become my friends, a few memories surface. For example, I heard that the students could not understand my speech patterns or those of my assistant. This may seem impossible now with the sort of homogeneity that radio and television have brought about in our language, but back in 1948 Southwestern Ontario did have a distinctive use of diphthongs that today can be heard only rarely. Then, too, Waterloo County still had areas dominated by "Dutchie" talk such as New Hamburg and Baden where "J" turned into "ch" as in "Vait chust a minute." There must have been distinctive speech rhythms too which I cannot recall.

My assistant and I arrived with a layer of University of Toronto speech (the catty called it mid-Atlantic) on top of Saskatchewan and Manitoba patterns, on top of Highland Scots with some Gaelic intonation (in my case) and in his, Lowland Scots. The only solution was provided by time. All of us probably modified our pitch and rhythms to become intelligible to the others, thus contributing to a new Southwestern Ontario linguistic phenomena.

Another reason for my inspiring distrust in my associates was— don't laugh—sartorial. After I had become more integrated into the faculty, a Lutheran layman gave me a direct hint about brightening up my wardrobe. We had to appear before the Kitchener-Waterloo public at various public functions, and apparently my appearance was too sombre. I was shocked because I thought I was really well-dressed, just like the upper-class ladies I had encountered in Toronto. In fact, my clothes had all been made in Toronto. By chance, a woman whose husband later became Governor-General was placed in the little study in the University of Toronto library which I had inhabited for a year or so, and we became friends. She had come back to university to do a graduate degree in philosophy, on top of her commitments as mother, wife, and (before long) political hostess. I recall her telling me she and her husband had decided to take the risk of going into politics and losing for a time the security of his income as a lawyer. Even without that motivation she would have been a careful manager of finances, and she introduced me to one of her resources, a tailor who worked only in the best materials which he kept on hand, and who loved to make women look nice. He, in turn, introduced me to a milliner, a refugee, who made hats that brought out one's best features and hid the worse. (We all wore hats then.) I realize now that he charged me only what he thought I could afford—which wasn't much—and not what the wives of CEOs would pay—but then I didn't ask any questions. Thus I arrived in Waterloo with a perfect wardrobe that I could have worn with assurance to Buckingham Palace—all black, grey, or beige with a bit of relief in cream or muted colours, and all in wool or silk with some cotton for warmer weather.

Some time ago when I visited a niece's family in San Francisco, I was taken to a concert of baroque opera, where the audience had stepped out of Toronto in the 1950s. There were the same faces above the same clothes, wool in the shades I have described, though not quite as smart as the suits MrLax had made for me. I had tapped into a social group like that which, in my time in Toronto had supported the symphony, and Sir Ernest MacMillan's choir, and all the other worthy causes of Old Toronto.

Well, it wouldn't do for Waterloo, so I did make myself a few new blouses and bought some attention-getting scarves. Again, I started to fit in—and perhaps the campus community changed a little its ideas of how women should appear in public.

I said I *made* clothes. Yes, I had a secret. In the 1930s my sister and I had taken over the sewing machine from my mother (who until then had by its means kept us decent) and we proceeded to make our clothes. My father, though he wouldn't have recognized the phrase, demanded of us a *bella figura*, the Italian ideal which means more than "well-dressed." Since we didn't have much money, we developed the skill to manage with very little, which stood me in good stead as I tried to meet the sartorial standards of my new home.

This might be a good point at which to stop and try to explain what we all looked like then. (I was shocked when a youngster looking at a photo of my sister and me said in surprise, "People in olden times looked just like us!" For me, olden times meant the 1830s; for her it meant the 1930s and '40s.)

As I walk through the halls today I try to recall how the students would have looked, in "olden times," but it is difficult. I think, in general, I can say that in 1948 they would have looked more "dressed up." A girl (not a young woman) would have worn a skirt, blouse, and some sort of jacket or cardigan, the men would have worn ties and something over their shirts—a jacket or cardigan or sleeveless sweater. There would not have been any jeans or trousers in colour or stripes or patterns. The girls would wear hats at the teas (compulsory events where they learned to be hostesses), and I think each man would have owned a hat, though he might not have worn it except when it was chilly. After all, he had to have something with which to acknowledge the presence of a lady.

I recently saw a man edging into his seat in a concert hall wearing a baseball cap without brim, which seems to be the latest variation on the baseball cap worn backwards. The rest of his attire would have been suitable for a gym in the 1940s—and '50s too. I think he was rather proud of himself as wearing the latest in menswear.

The women at the concert wore no hats, of course, and largely long skirts—there is some uncertainty at the moment about the claims of long or short as *le dernier cri*. Perhaps there were some in black tights in short or very short skirts. Colours were muted though I saw a smart checked wool jacket on a friend's wife. The friend was in a grey warm shirt with some sort of vest thing—and I don't think he had a tie, but since I knew his ancestors were Quakers that didn't surprise me.

I should add that back in 1948 there would not, I think, have been any long, straight hair. Practically every girl on campus would have waves, not regimented ones as in the earlier *marcel* but easy waves that made her look pretty rather than exotic. And she would have been very carefully, not dramatically made up. In later years the Avon lady used to make regular visits to the women's residences to replenish the supplies of cosmetics.

If my narrative lasts until the late 1960s, I may have occasion to chart the changes that resulted in the easy, uncomplicated look of jeans and sweatshirts and T-shirts with saucy or philosophical or commercial messages and pictures that identify the young women on campus today.

As an addendum I should say that the men on campus in the 1940s and early '50s would had haircuts with short back and sides. Only a visiting professor from Europe would have had his hair a bit longer at the back. Practically all the men were clean shaven too.

9

UNIVERSITY COMMUNITIES CAN SHOW many diverse examples of humanity even today, but the upheavals of the war and consequent movement of people made life on campuses even more interesting in the late 1940s and early '50s. I know that my acquaintance with the faculty and staff of Waterloo College, and with other groups close to the life of the place, gave me a liberal education in the study of mankind, and of womankind as well (but not as much since the faculty and student-body of the time was predominantly male).

In the forty-five years since I first arrived in Waterloo, academics have found new ways to name things. We didn't think in terms of racism, elitism, gender bias, etc. at Waterloo College. But even by today's standards, I think the college wouldn't look too bad. My own appointment as head of a department suggests that the glass ceiling was relatively high. It was about forty years before we had a female president, but there was no problem with hiring and promoting women. At least one prominent faculty member was known to be gay (though that adjective was still to the general public only a synonym for merry, jolly). The subject was carefully avoided when I arrived. Trudeau had not yet come along to get the law out of the bedrooms of the nation—but the gentleman concerned seemed happy in his lifestyle and in the wealth which he had inherited. When I was told he had been an international secretary for Rotary, I was properly unimpressed as being one who felt superior to all that, having read Sinclair Lewis. However, when he told me that Mrs. James Joyce used to give him afternoon tea in Zurich, I began to be impressed. (He liked her a lot but didn't think much of James.) When I ate at his table—where he was chaperoned by an elderly aunt and female cousin—and was told the silver side plates had once belonged to the mother of King Farouk of Egypt, I realized Rotary was not all that dull. (King Farouk's mother happened to be hard up when our host was in Cairo.)

I must add that when Gerald Hagey arrived on campus as president, he ended our friend's connection with the college, and at that time there was no cohort of gays and lesbians to picket the place. Hagey also objected to another situation, also gender-related but somewhat different. One faculty member had been enduring the kind of bad pregnancy that required her to spend several months in bed. Rather than give up her classes (she had financial responsibilities), she met the students in her home which was almost on campus, and taught her class reclining elegantly on something like a *chaise longue*. The students didn't seem to mind, but the new president did. Time resolved the problem, but the mother-to-be concerned still hasn't forgotten what she thought was uncalled for prudery. She was of European origin, while our president was very much of the older school of people raised in Ontario. Because of the mixture of ethnicities in the faculty and in the student body, it might be expected that there would be examples of prejudice carried out from the old land, if not native to this country, but I can recall very little. With our large body of Germans, dating from early in the history of the college up to the post-war period when we had an influx of ex-members of the army and German civilians into our student body, one might expect anti-Semitism. I can recall hearing only one anti-Semitic remark in my time at the college and university. It was repeated to me as coming from a young professor of Classics who would have been a schoolboy in Germany in Hitler's time. When he was told of the help he could receive from our audio-visual director in preparing slides for his classes he replied, "I'll have nothing to do with that Austrian Jew." True, the director was from Vienna, but had remained there untouched after the Anschluss (i.e., the 1938 annexation of Austria into the Third Reich) in spite of the Nuremberg laws. (His wife teased him that his alien aspect came from genes left behind in Bohemia by marauders from the east.)

The wife of one of our ex-students told me that, while growing up in Kitchener as a member of a Jewish family, she had felt a good deal of prejudice, but I think such prejudice became less common as more and more was learned of the horrors of the Nazi programme

of extermination, and especially unacceptable on a college or university campus. One reason for the sensitized climate on our campus may have been the fact that a professor at the seminary, Leupold,
a doctor of music from Berlin, had a Jewish father who had been a
church organist. His mother, a church soloist, had been *echt Deutsch*
(a "real" or "true" German). The father had been fortunate enough
to die before they came for him, the mother remained safely in Germany until after the war, while the son, now a Lutheran clergyman,
was somehow removed from danger and sent by the church to minister to a congregation in one of the less urban areas of Ontario. He
rarely referred to his former parishioners, but I have known him to
permit himself a smile as he thought of their simplicity which must
have been a great surprise to a sophisticated Berliner. I seem to
remember seeing a house in that area garlanded for some patriot or
church celebration, and I was told the people had kept up customs
inherited from their forbears in out-of-the-way parishes in the old
land.

A member of a famous campus family—his father had been head
of the seminary—told me he was sure that they had once been Jews,
called Klein. I gathered that the gentleman who had defended our
performance of *The Importance of Being Earnest* was quite right
when he pointed out that baptism had at one time been an entrance
into a new life for many, not just for people tracing their origin to a
handbag (as it was in Wilde's play).

For examples of "racism" in the terms of today, we should look
at the treatment of people who were obviously not "white" and
there too I found at the time nothing that I could call unjust, or
unfair, or unkind. There were very few Asians. A look at the history of the time will tell you why, but we had students from areas
where there were Lutheran missions, especially in Africa and in
what is now Guyana.

There were two notable students from Africa, a man and a
woman, both, I think, from Ghana. I am sure that the man, Seth
Bansa, was Ghanian, and since he told me on a fairly recent visit to
Waterloo that the woman, Mercy Okum had visited him with her
children to recall old times in Waterloo, she couldn't have lived too
far away. Seth is now blind from glaucoma, and less active than he

would like to be, but in the past he and his wife Olive were among the makers of the new Liberia where they helped to build up a university and were close to the rulers of the time. That is, before the civil war in which all of their work was destroyed and they were very lucky to get back to Ghana with their lives. Most of their children except, I think, one are successfully settled in the United States (I saw their photos) and Seth and Olive are able to visit them for prolonged periods.

Mercy was a tall, regal chief's daughter who quite naturally left her luggage and appurtenances to be picked up and carried by the other girls in the residence. She got a touch of TB and spent some time at the sanatorium in Freeport. When I visited her I was received as if by the late Queen Mary, not really condescendingly but *de haut en bas*. I was glad to know her life in Africa had turned out well.

The students from Guyana were almost all of Indian origin and had been recruited by Lutheran missionaries as had the Africans. Not too long after I arrived in Waterloo, Cheddi Jagan won an election, and then had problems with the British who found him too far to the left. My first Guyanese student told me he was a friend of Cheddi and hoped for his success. Our ex-student has recently written the story of his life which he let me read. He became a lawyer and dealt on the side in real estate, becoming comfortably well-off and establishing himself in the local community. His wife is the sister of one of our post-war students from Germany.

I shall not continue to give examples, but want to establish that Waterloo College had an admirably relaxed atmosphere where students, faculty, and staff of many levels of society and diverse ethnic backgrounds felt an ease and warmth that they have not forgotten— nor have I, because I still feel that they are part of a family of which I had the privilege to be a member.

In spite of all I have said here, I came under suspicion of racism several times and each time felt a certain amount of rejection. The story has to do with my responsibility for maintaining standards. One of my problems arose because a student from Guyana didn't realize that an *aegrotat* mark (given if the student proved illness at an examination) would be the mark he had received for term work. This poor soul had passed nothing during the term, and when he vomited over his examination paper and claimed an "aegrotat" he got the mark he had earned. Several congregations were told about my hardness of heart and unfairness.

Two other situations were not as clear cut. Both involved faculty members in the English department who didn't meet their classes. The first was Jewish. The head of University College in Toronto had phoned me to ask me to hire him. I should have known that here was a case of a fellow who just wasn't "cutting it" anywhere in spite of his lovable nature. When he went to take his PhD generals (comprehensive exams), he collapsed and renounced the struggle to the doctorate in spite of my policy of not renewing contracts for those who were not progressing to the final degree. That he wrote obscene remarks on students' essays didn't enter into it because we were remarkably tolerant in those days. Then I received pathetic notes from his students asking, "Where is our professor?" When we didn't renew his contract, he went about telling of our anti-Semitism until Windsor hired him. At the Learneds that year some people were cool to me, but warmed up later when he ran away from Windsor with one of his students, leaving a long-suffering wife and son. In the meantime he had told us before he left us that he would be giving a paper at the Learneds in Vancouver on a subject something like "The Genitals of Othello." On the plane he tried to write it, but the day it was to be delivered he was ill. His friends at last said, "Poor X, he didn't make it, did he?"

The other personnel problem attributed to racism was Indian, bright, entertaining, but he too didn't meet his classes. His poor father in India used to telephone him to exhort him to work hard, but somehow he couldn't get it together. The dean lost patience and gave him an ultimatum: if he missed another class he would not get the promotion promised him. Sure enough he ran out of gas on the highway from Guelph where he lived and the dean lowered the boom. (No, he wasn't fired.) The disappointed man made the circuit of nearby universities, lecturing persuasively on our racism— and this time people were really cool to me at the Learneds. I was quite unpopular until I received a letter from the head of the department that had hired him, "How did you get X to meet his classes? I telephoned back (one never puts it in writing!) to explain that I couldn't get X to meet his classes—that was the trouble—and X faded out of academic life.

And could there be any accusations of prejudice in connection with our common and garden-variety students, drawn from in and around the Twin Cities? At first there was some sensitivity in those who spoke the language of Southern Ontario. People to whom I was introduced would say, "Oh, you're an English teacher. I'll have to watch how I talk." I gathered that generations of school teachers had made them aware of their linguistic shortcomings, but actually I heard and read very little that was unacceptable English. One student who had maintained a good standard in all his work broke back into mixed numbers and cases when he spoke to me at our graduation ceremonies, and I realized that the mother tongue—which in his case was really a dialect of some British origin in which "you was" was standard is very hard to leave behind.

I soon gave up thinking of stereotypes in our Canadian students. One day when I was talking about Yeats, a Mennonite student said teasingly, "You sound just like my Irish grandmother." I had wondered where he had got his sense of humour. And another student who took only his first two years with us, leaving us for the University of Toronto, told me that his four grandparents had been from four quite distinct European and I think mid-Eastern cultures.

I was getting a liberal education.

10

Our students also got a liberal education from the mingling of nationalities on our campus. The most obvious influence was of course German. At happy gatherings, students of all races would sing songs such as "Muss ich denn," perhaps not understanding many of the words but responding to the spirit, especially with German Christmas music. When the University of Waterloo took over our name, our songs disappeared too, but have been resurrected, I understand, at the local Oktoberfest. Incidentally, Oktoberfest was to a great degree inspired by our ex-public relations man of whom there will be more later if I reach the days of President Villaume.

Perhaps I could write of just a few of the ex-soldiers who came to us from Germany to make a new life. The *hausvater* I have mentioned who drove a little Austin had been a Canadian army chaplain, part of whose duties were carried out in prisoner-of-war camps in Canada, but I don't know of any connection between him and the war veterans who became our students because he never talked about his war-time experiences to me, though he was quite open about other things. I don't know if we had a larger percentage of German students than did other universities, but it is reasonable to suppose that there would be some word-of-mouth information about a place where Germans would find some appreciation of the literature and landscape of the fatherland. I'll mention just two or three examples.

One of the students from Germany was a very large young man. He assured me he hadn't been in the ss—his army duties had consisted in twirling a little dial to aim an anti-aircraft gun. The heavy shells, he said, were man-handled into the weapon by a puny little chap, an example, he implied, of the usual stupidity of officialdom of all stripes. He had a ready laugh and an air of good fellowship.

He had been at Heidelberg after the war and there he was denazified. He described it as having had to think things through and change his ideas in the light of what he learned. (He was no more specific than I have been, but I gathered that part of his re-education was the formation of a new attitude to Jews.) He found it hard to absorb still more re-education as we presented the philosophy in works of English and American and Canadian literature. For example, I recall that the New England Transcendentalists bothered him a lot because he couldn't square them with what he had studied as Transcendentalism at Heidelberg. Emerson and Thoreau seemed far from Kant and Schelling.

After he obtained a doctorate he returned to our German department as a colleague. Shortly after his retirement, he died in Germany where he and his wife had, I think, retained a house, and where they spent their vacations.

Always he was a soldier, and a German soldier. When we had the service of remembrance on November 11, he was there, recalling, I am sure, many lost *Kameraden*: he had served on the Russian front.

One of my memories of him is of a late afternoon in the faculty lounge where several Canadians were chatting about their martial careers. One told how he patrolled the sky over the St. Lawrence looking for enemy submarines, with no luck until the day when, by mistake, he dropped a charge all too near to a French-Canadian fisherman who raised hell with the authorities about the "attack." Another told how his unit blew the lightship out of Halifax harbour in target practice. Klaus listened in wonderment until at last he broke out, "How *could* we have lost the war!" The answer was, apart from the fact that our side tended to reminisce about their cock-ups rather than their triumphs, that we had Hitler and Roosevelt on our side: Hitler with his astonishing lapses of judgement, and Roosevelt with his endless stream of *matériel*, but no one wanted to spoil the fun by mentioning that.

I'd like to detour here to retell the story I enjoyed most that afternoon. One ex-soldier told of the early Canadian expedition to Iceland. I hadn't heard of it, but it had been part of the attempts to protect the island from invasion. According to our friend, the main problem for the Canadians was lack of female company, which they hoped to remedy by putting on a big dance and inviting all the young women to attend. On the designated night, the soldiers were watching the doors eagerly waiting for the ladies to arrive. In they came, the Icelandic beauties, each of them accompanied by her *father*.

Speaking of Iceland, and to continue detouring: once in Saskatoon I was waiting for a streetcar in the late 1930s. Two tall, thin ladies in old-fashioned suits and hats stood in front of me. I believe they even had umbrellas. First lady firmly: "There are *no* jails in Iceland." Second lady just as firmly: "There are no *bad* people in Iceland." Things changed when the Americans arrived on the island, I am told.

And one more story before we get back on the track. On the occasion of the anniversary of the landing in Normandy, a friend of mine was telephoned by the BBC a few years ago for his recollections of the actual event. He told them that, when his unit came ashore, they were faced with very challenging sand dunes. His heavily laden men were scrambling and sliding while he and his sergeant major easily made it to the top to find a German gun nest not far away, all the members thereby gazing open-mouthed at the sight of two Englishmen apparently advancing on them alone. "We'll have to keep going," said my friend, so they went on until the Germans were just a few paces away. In his pocket my friend had, naturally, a packet of cigarettes which he pulled out and tossed to the nearest German. The packet was handed around, and the lot of them surrendered. "But we had a bad time a few days later," said my friend, reflectively. Since the BBC saw fit not to use such an uninteresting story, I take advantage of this chance to record it to demonstrate that German soldiers are not all stereotypes. There is a connection with my main story too. Our German ex-student and colleague had been among those I mentioned earlier who were lucky enough to fall into the hands of the British at the end of the war.

Before I leave him I want to tell of the lecture on Bertolt Brecht. Each year I ran a course on world literature, with the lectures given by experts from relevant departments. I had asked Klaus to speak on Brecht, but had warned him that the class might be visited by young men in black leather jackets with trouble on their minds in case they heard something other than the East German line of propaganda. I don't know where they came from but I knew they existed because once they had come to barrack my lecture on *For Whom the Bells Tolls* in Toronto (on that occasion they were there to shout down any defence of Hemingway). We now know that Hemingway had got the situation in Spain down only too well: Stalin *was* using the Civil War to exterminate other leftist groups, but at that time around 1947 I didn't know why the book was politically incorrect in some circles. I just discussed it as a novel, and was not mobbed by the militant Left. Well, on the evening of the lecture on Brecht they were there, sitting among our regular students. Klaus told me afterwards that he spotted them at once and was ready. He began with a summary of Brecht's financial assets, stashed away in various capitalist banks, and he felt the atmosphere deflate as he went on. At the intermission our visitors left. The fact that the speaker was a great many inches taller and some pounds heavier than any of them—and looked as if he could take care of himself—may have had something to do with their collapse of interest in the lecture.

The German soldier had become one of us, but his widow told me that, after his death, she found a paper in his desk on which he had written only the sentence, "I shall never understand this country."

A very different German war veteran comes next to my mind; he had left school to join the army, and had been taken prisoner in North Africa. I think he still had trouble believing it had happened. The African Korps was still for him totally invincible. Whenever he came to my office to pick up an essay, we seemed to get into a conversation about his experiences. He had been totally taken in by Nazi teachings and now he had to square his ideas with what he was slowly learning in Canada. Little by little he recognized German weaknesses. Perhaps, for instance, the *esprit de corps* had *not* held to the end. One day he asked, "What would you think of fourteen-year-olds shooting their officers?" I gathered that, when things fell apart, some of the youths turned on the wielders of army discipline. Some years later he telephoned me to convey a simple greeting—he had been visiting in this area and had thought of me. In the background I could hear the usual noises Canadian children make when their elders are occupied for a moment, and he turned around to shout at them like any indulgent, but exasperated Canadian father. I assumed that most of his ghosts were at rest.

The other German student I shall recall here also had ghosts, associated with the Russian front. He too had assumed that the *Wehrmacht* was invincible—so technically advanced, so tactically superior. "We mowed them down, and they kept coming," he said in horror. "They kept coming, wave after wave." I have forgotten whether he said he was wounded and thus removed from the nightmare. When I first knew him he had taken refuge in Buddhism. By chance I saw him again a couple of years ago, a steady, happy retiree who had found his life in teaching, and like the others had learned to live between two cultures, finally leaning more to the new.

I have already said that I saw very little anti-Semitism on campus. In fact I do not recall any discussion of the fate of German Jews, but I'd like to mention here two remarks which should come later in the story, because one came from a science professor, hired after we became independent. He was said to have worked with Werner Heisenberg at one time, and during the war was involved in the production of rocket fuel. One day I was reading in the faculty lounge when he came in. I didn't greet him at once, being involved in my book, and was startled to hear him say, "Dr. Roy, I swear to you, I didn't know." Someone else must have come in, saving me from a reply, happily, since I don't know how I could have avoided revealing my disbelief. Was it really possible for someone to be so caught up in his research that he hadn't noticed that there were no longer any Jewish colleagues?

The other remark was made by my medical doctor, the wife of one of our Canadian professors. She was German, and had come up through years of Nazi indoctrination as a school girl, university student, and later as a practising physician. She had studied for a time at Innsbruck. Although I never heard her mention the students, brother and sister, who were decapitated there for anti-Nazi activities, she must have known of them, and absorbed the warning from their fate. She told me that just before war broke out she had gone with some friends for a holiday in the mountains. One of the young men was killed in a fall, but she assured me that they could not really mourn for him because they knew he would be spared the future that they feared for themselves: the difficult position of being anti-Nazi in Germany. When she became a physician, she was assigned to work in a v.d. clinic (we now say "sexually transmitted diseases") and told me that she had wondered about the devastation that would ensue should a new strain of venereal diseases develop that would be incurable by such means as they then had. She didn't live to see the AIDS epidemic. At another time she told me she was required to assist in a mandatory abortion for a slave labourer. When she was in the operating room she couldn't go on and managed to be excused, "I knew there was life there," she said.

She was a "caring," sensitive woman, yet one day when she was grumbling to herself about her father's shortcomings—he was going to quacks instead of doctors, etc.—I was horrified to hear her say, "And he was helping Jews." I didn't inquire further because I didn't think she intended me to overhear, but I realized that if he had really been aiding Jews to escape the gas chambers, his whole family would have been in danger. It made me wonder whether we have any right to require others to be heroes when we have never been tried in a similar fashion. I was learning more about the complexities of being human.

II

Nᴏᴛ ᴀʟʟ Gᴇʀᴍᴀɴ ɪɴꜰʟᴜᴇɴᴄᴇꜱ ᴏɴ ᴄᴀᴍᴘᴜꜱ and in the community were as unsettling as those just presented. For a time after the 1939–45 war, it was possible to have a happy and interesting life in Kitchener and Waterloo speaking nothing but German. One of the movie theatres ran a steady offering of German films. I managed to see a lot of them, laughing at the comedies which tended to end in friendly punch-ups at gatherings featuring young women in dirndls and young men with Tyrolean hats, though I sometimes caught examples of more ambitious film-making during the war. One was a film based in Prague, and starring an actress who was known as the "wasser nise" because in so many of her films she was submerged in various bodies of water. Another was based on Rilke's story of Cornet Christopher Rilke's life and death. In that connection I was amazed to hear a woman, long a local resident, tell me how as a student she had bicycled a considerable distance one day to have a visit with Lou Andreas-Salome, the friend of Rilke and others whom I had thought of as existing only in the faraway past. The visit was not too interesting, she said, but it did bring Nietzsche and Rilke somehow into our own time.

She was most annoyed to learn that a number of the Germans who were clustered around our college had a lecture series in German on our campus, given by a professor from Toronto. The subject was Shakespeare. When I asked why it was necessary to import someone to speak on that subject, I was told seriously that Shakespeare was much better in German than in English, so a German speaker would understand him better than someone who read him in the original language. It is true that many German translators of the English bard were famous in their own right, but I couldn't believe that they had improved on Elizabethan English, though I was assured that it was so. Now I realize I should have been thankful that anyone was interested in Shakespeare. Before the pitching of Stratford's tent theatre, Shakespeare's plays had bored generations of Ontario grade thirteen students—with only a few rare exceptions.

I earlier mentioned the friend I had met in Banff whom I found on the college faculty. He had settled into a new house on Albert Street with his newish wife, and his mother and brothers and their families were arriving from Germany to join him. In those days we didn't inquire closely into the origins of our colleagues, and very few volunteered information about themselves, but one heard rumours. It was said that my friend came from a family in Germany with strong ideas about caring for nature and the environment. They had set up some sort of business in accord with their principles and, in spite of themselves, had done very well. Not long ago I read in an article by Frederick Crews (*New York Review of Books*, October 3, 1996), a mention of a pre-war German group, "the left-liberal Lebens-reform movement, who were typically fond of rural communes, vegetarianism, alternative medicine, nudism, and the like." That sounds a bit like my friend; he had for a time belonged to a Canadian commune (urban) but I had no evidence of the nudism.

When they all arrived in Canada, the father had been dead for some time. He had been some sort of government official and there was a "von" floating around in their name. One of the brothers used it, I believe, but my friend didn't make any obvious claim to nobility. To my mind his mother was the interesting one. She was English and her accent and her attitudes placed her at a pretty high level in the social hierarchy: I'd say that she could have met Lady Passfield as an equal—perhaps she had. She paid no attention to other people's opinions of her—I recall that she rolled her own cigarettes (or was that the cousin of Lord Onslow I met a long time ago on a farm near Niagara?). Her son told me she had listened to the BBC all through the war and, what was more, told everyone what she had heard. My friend said his blood ran cold whenever he thought of it. When the end came it was she who had got the family to safety—and finally they joined their Canadian member.

My friend had become a pillar of our German department. My only recollection of his academic career with us is of seeing him at a seminar in his own home with the students seated on the floor around him. Usually he was holding forth on the Apollonian and the Dionysian so that may have been the subject being discussed. I recall especially one student, a girl with her long blonde hair wrapped around her head, completely lost in contemplation of the ideas or of the professor, but I think the worshipping stopped there.

My friend had been interested in agriculture at one time, and had learned somewhere that if you want to have a good lawn you should grow rye for several years and dig it into the soil. Thus, on a street of lawns built up of costly turf, there was this little field of rye which may not have appealed to the neighbours. On Sundays when good Lutherans were passing by on their way to church, they saw my friend, a somewhat less than Apollonian figure, in over-large shorts, attending to his farming. When he left (I don't know if it was his idea or the dean's) he took some of the eccentric and exotic side of the campus family with him—but there was plenty left.

We were not the only college to have German or Austrian aristocrats in our midst: I once met a von Richthofen in Edmonton, and though, I think, not ennobled there was a family connection of Thomas Mann's wife at the University of Waterloo—at least so I was told. But we had our share. A number of refugees or "displaced persons" had been Baltic barons who did not wait for the Russians to arrive. They even had some sort of association here. Mrs. Aksim, whom I shall describe later, was invited to join, but she was quite scornful of the idea. (*She* was *Russian*; it was only her husband who was Estonian.) I recognized one of the barons in an extension class one Saturday morning, but soon saw that his English was not equal to the task of comprehending the lecture. I wonder what happened to him. He *could*, of course, take German courses but an English credit was required for graduation. I saw him briefly later when I visited our lady from Prague in the hospital when she had her tonsils removed. It was clear that they were good friends.

The lady from Prague enlivened our campus, and won the hearts of faculty and fellow students. Her father was a baron, and an amateur astronomer. She recalled being a child spending nights with the telescope. Her mother died during the war because they had no sulfa drugs (were they only for the troops?). Our "baroness" had married the son of the chief city engineer of Prague. He was declared missing on the Russian front. I hope she will tell us how she herself got out of Russian hands and into our midst. All I know is one story with a point. A young Russian officer had been telling her how the Soviet system guaranteed equality. As they moved to the dance floor she said, "And shall I lead?" Fortunately he thought it a joke, but it shows that she would take a chance.

She joined in all the important student activities. Though she must have been a bit older than the rest, they felt that she was one of them, and I suspect several of our male students learned something about sophisticated European women from her. Now she tells us that on our campus she felt, for the first time since the Russians came, that someone cared about her. Though she later went to the USA and joined the faculty of a well-known college, she has kept her Canadian citizenship as a sort of thank-you for the welcome we gave her. I still keep in touch with her through Christmas greetings, and at one time through long telephone calls made when she visited friends who lived here (until recently).

I have mentioned Mrs. Aksim before, but now I want to convey something of what she meant to the college. Her house was just off the edge of the campus on Bricker Avenue. On fine summer days there was coffee for anyone who came in the open-sided summer house at the end of the garden. At other times there was hospitality in the homey living room. Her children brought in their friends, the faculty and their families dropped in, neighbours came and went. When her children left, Mrs. Aksim took in student boarders so they and *their* friends maintained the easy, open atmosphere of a Russian home—perhaps a little cluttered, with something going on all the time in a cheerful confusion.

Yes, Russian, though the reigning language was supposed to be German, and there was some scorn for anyone who did not speak that tongue correctly and fluently, but the atmosphere was Russian. As with others of our campus friends from overseas, Mrs. Aksim never spoke to me of her life in the old land, and the little I know was acquired after her death when I was asked to write something about her in the alumni magazine. Her home was on an estate next to that of the unfortunate prince in *War and Peace*. I do not recall if it was her father or grandfather (surely the latter?) who came to work on the estate after a time of living in the woods as a mysterious German refugee. No one seems to know from what exactly he had run, but there were plenty of risings and retaliations at the time to account for flight. The heir to the estate was an only child, an unmarried daughter, who in time married the man from the forest, the Waldmann, which, I think, became their name. Anton Chekhov could have written the script for this family's life.

Our Mrs. Aksim was brought up in what had become a somewhat strict German family, but spent as much of her time as possible with the Russian staff and servants, absorbing the language, the gestures, and the outlook of a more colourful world. She once told me that the people who educated her had said, "A woman must know everything," so she was exposed to branches of learning that in the past were reserved for men. I gathered that this education was in Moscow. At her funeral service, the officiant who was her son-in-law preached from one of the many texts referring to being a stranger in a strange land. He had detected her distinguishing quality. She was, among us, unfailing in generosity, always available, but we were always foreign, speaking a poor German, or a poorish Russian, reading by choice things that did not measure up to Tolstoy or Dostoevsky—or Goethe or Schiller for that matter.

She had a special group of friends (we were all her friends, of course) whom she called "the old ladies." (Since she herself died at nearly 96, looking twenty years younger, she may have been close to the eldest in the group.) They read aloud at some of their gatherings, and local Canadians who wanted to improve their German joined them. I was invited to practise the language too, and read with her a little book by Rilke. I know that she was sorry for me because I was so ill-educated. I found her so interesting that I persevered, to hear her say, a little before her death, "You are my oldest friend here." She was perfectly aware of the double meaning which reminded me that I was no longer young, while still conveying some regard, if not affection. Slim, hair still dark, eyes alert, mind still questing and making quick judgements, comparisons, distinctions, amused always by the ironies of the distance between intentions and realities: she was fascinating until the end.

Her daughter told me that her mother had seen her sister marry
the man she herself loved, and in her turn she married an Estonian
clergyman and went off to the south where she had her children and
lived as a pastor's wife. She told me once of being taken to a
tribesman's home where the men in striped hard-woven woollen
trousers sat on the floor eating strawberry jam and rose petals, a
glimpse for me of the wild world that claimed Lermontov, though
I was probably romanticizing the whole thing with my weak grasp
of geography.

When the Russian system broke down in revolution, her husband was arrested as a member of the ruling class, and the family
lived as best it could. Mrs. Aksim told me she managed to buy a
cow (or trade something for it) and one way and another kept the
children alive. A servant had wanted to kill them because they spoke
German but was somehow persuaded to desist. At last the father
managed to get to Estonia, and his wife and family, huddled in freight
cars with only what they could carry (which meant fine rugs, brought
for warmth and comfort, and jewellery hidden in the mother's abun-
dant hair), were able to follow him.

The father had visited Canada on a sort of mission to Estonian
Lutheran churches. His grandsons think the visits had something to
do with Estonian nationalism as well as with ecclesiastical business. Now, he was somehow offered a post at Waterloo College or
at the Seminary—or both—and the family joined him. Unfortunately,
after all their ordeals, their peace didn't last long. The father died suddenly of a heart condition (inherited by his sons, I believe) and once
again the family had to exist alone, this time on a miniscule pen-
sion from the church. The Russian aristocrat did any odd jobs available, raised a necessary garden for food, and still remained resilient,
meeting the judge's wife and the janitor's wife on the same plane,
still amused at "what fools these mortals be." I have a photo of her
dancing with the judge at her granddaughter's wedding, still erect,
graceful, aristocratic. The campus could not help reflecting her personality and her intelligence.

She became even closer to us when she was made house mother
in the first real residence in the old Devitt house which was now ren-
ovated once more. Some of her living-room furniture came with

her, I think, because the atmosphere of her house was recreated in the room where she had coffee hour in front of a plant-filled window. The girls, naturally, tried to evade her careful chaperonage and her advice. I have heard at least one story of the male student who dived under the bed when she arrived to look in on the proper inhabitant of the room, and stayed there during a long and pleasant chat, to escape safely when it was over. The men's residence was not very far away.

When a young man was to call for a resident, the girl tried to be on hand to greet him, introduce him to the house mother, and escape. If Mrs. Aksim was left to entertain him on her own, she might, if he was a regular caller, bring the conversation around to his intentions and his prospects, which by the 1950s was regarded by Canadian girls as the best way to discourage a potential "boy-friend."

When she returned to her Bricker Avenue home, the connection with the campus continued since she took in faculty and students as boarders and taught Russian to any who wished to learn, especially to two members of the history department, one of whom wrote a thesis, later a book, on a Russian theme. I believe they loved her—and maybe I did too—but she kept herself apart, as her son-in-law said at her funeral, walking about in the Moscow in her head, a Moscow without highrises, where they had not yet blown up the churches and the great cathedral, a Moscow in the ferment of science, and art, and politics which seemed to be changing it into a leading part of intellectual and cultural Europe. The change came but as we know, it was not quite as expected.

The point of all this is that with a small faculty and a not very numerous student body the college was easily influenced by a strong personality, and the vaguely European atmosphere on campus, difficult to define yet distinct, owed quite a bit to Mrs. Aksim.

12

THE AKSIMS HAD COME TO WATERLOO COLLEGE because of the Lutheran connection, but how had she, a Russian, come to be

Lutheran? And other of our non-German students and friends, how
did *they* happen to be Lutheran? For some the answer lay in migra-
tion at the time of the counter-reformation. Reformed Christians
on the edges of areas being won back by the church pushed north and
east to find a refuge. I recall that Mrs. Aksim's daughter once told
me that part of her mother's ancestry had followed from Italy the old
trade route of the Hanseatic League, which as we know extended
into territory that became Russian. A policy of welcoming outsiders
who could help in the development of Russia's economy and trade
would help to explain how, in an Orthodox land, little cells of Lutherans could be found. A former colleague for instance, a refugee, was,
like her mother, an Orthodox Ukrainian, while her father had been
head of a Lutheran college in the Ukraine. (An early Mennonite
bishop in Waterloo County said that his people had been among the
Anabaptists who also fled north to escape the counter-reformation
in Northern Italy.)

We know the orthodoxy of Russia came from the Eastern Roman
Empire. But how did most of the original inhabitants across the rest
of the northern part of Europe happen to become Lutheran? Because
of the Teutonic Knights, said my Estonian friends. Their manner of
evangelizing the northern peoples was never forgotten, and when
the chance came to cast off the creed they had imposed, the people
in the Baltic lands eagerly embraced it.

Their Lutheranism brought many Estonian and Latvian students
and some faculty members to the exotic mix that was our campus
population. One of them, who became head of our political science
department, told us of a banquet at which he was an honoured guest
after the collapse of the Russian hegemony over the Baltic states.
"And if they had caught me there just a short time before," he said,
"they would have shot me." A younger member of the same department made many visits to Estonia and to Russia in the Gorbachev
era and described the confusion and incomprehension in what should
have been centre of Moscow decision making. "What shall we do?"
they asked him. He did not stop to try to advise them. His business
was with the Estonians who were preparing for independence and
anticipating its problems. Aside we might note that Canadians of
Estonian roots had been supporting their countrymen pretty well

all through the cold war and were ready to help when the time came. Not too long ago I met one of our graduates, a chaplain in our armed forces, resplendent in his clerical clothing. He told me he was just back from Estonia where he had organized their military chaplaincy. Our Estonian students did not waste their time. They were going to be ready to take the positions in Canadian life they or their families had known in the world before 1939. They looked the part too, well groomed, making the most of their appearance. I recall one young woman writing a disgusted critique of the poem about the attractions of a lady in dishabille. "The author liked a messy girl," she declared. Another told me she learned English by memorizing the dictionary, as if it were a quite normal undertaking.

I am going to dwell on the story of one Estonian couple who became my good friends, partly because it will testify to the cultural influence on us of these "newcomers," as they called themselves. My connection with them also had an unintended influence on the decision of the Lutheran Synod not to give up the college to the new University of Waterloo.

I had not been long at the college before I became aware of the fact that my vocal cords were not going to stand up to the task of lecturing all day, day after day, unless I took some steps to strengthen them. I was told of a newcomer who was giving voice lessons in town, a former opera singer from Estonia. I made an appointment and was greeted by a direct, no-nonsense little lady who understood at once what the problem was and put me on a strict regime of breathing exercises before she would even think of treating the voice. Hella Teder herself was not only a graduate of the music conservatory, but had also been sent by the state to study *bel canto* in Italy, and had then been given a post in the Estonian opera company. I have seen a photo of her, costumed as Carmen, and she told of playing the child in *Boris*, I believe with Feodor Chaliapin.

She was not too popular with local music teachers, who invited her to come and speak to them on how to teach singing, because she intimated that without years of study of music in general, and of the voice in particular, you could not presume to teach. Some pupils must have been frightened away by her standards. "Do you want to sing in church basements?" she would ask neophytes, and if the answer was "yes," she would have nothing to do with them. As soon as I was enrolled as a pupil, I was forbidden to sing in public—not that I intended to—but she relented when I asked if I might join the ladies' choir that sang vespers each Sunday in our parish church.

Teder treated each voice differently, working on attaining an even register and eventually a "singing" legato on which she could build. I found that my troubles in lecturing soon cleared up, and I was on the way to enjoying years of *lieder* and art songs with Hella and her husband. I should add that one of her students, a soprano, was employed by a Finnish opera company for a time, and another, a baritone, sold the house he inherited when his parents died and went back to Germany to try his luck in opera there, with some success, I am told, so she seems to have been on the right track.

For years I had two lessons each week, one of exercises, and one of singing. The lessons were only a half hour since she insisted that until the vocal instrument was strong, any longer time could do serious damage. Her husband, who was a more-than-competent pianist, didn't seem to mind acting as accompanist to our attempts at Schubert or Mozart. My singing lesson was arranged to be the last on Friday evenings so that when it was over we could relax with coffee and conversation. They were interested in everything that went on at "their" Lutheran college so I came to confide in them a great deal that I would not have told anyone else, especially as events moved towards the final disruption resulting in two universities. In turn they told me a great deal about their 1939–45 war—first under the Russian invasion and later under the Germans.

Although the husband had become a pianist, he had sensibly also studied economics and held a post in the Department of Finance so that their world had included figures from the state opera, and others from the government administration. When I think about it now, I wonder why I never asked them anything about the years of political experiments that had preceded the war. A great deal of our chat came back to the Russian occupation. I now know that they were telling only the truth when they described the evictions and murders of the time. Hella Teder had once had a vision in which she saw her sister's husband beaten to death on a forced march to exile, a vision that was later corroborated. (I came to be unsurprised by stories of second sight and other psychic phenomena from these northern people.)

For a time the husband had to remain at his post in Finance but with a Russian co-worker. One of their jobs was forecasting economic trends, with the prospect of being shot if they were proved wrong. Once, when my friend asked in exasperation how one could tell what was going to happen to the economy, the Russian replied, "I always consult Professor Ceiling," with a mock-despairing upwards look. (He could not say he asked "the good Lord" of course.) One wonders to what extent the troubles of the Russian economy in later years might have been owing to "Professor Ceiling." When the Germans were advancing into Estonia, the Russians made further sweeps of those who might not be totally reliable as allies. My friend was called for by an ambulance that sped him to a hospital where he was quickly given a false name and watched in bandages until the Germans arrived. An Estonian underground, including the doctors, had organized to save a few key people that way.

Hella and her opera colleagues were mobilized to dig trenches in the path of the Germans. On the way they came on a seemingly deserted house; inside was a dead woman. The Communist guards said, "Dig a hole and throw her in," but one of them, an Estonian (yes, there were quislings there too) said, "No. We'll bury an Estonian woman the Estonian way," and soon the opera group stood around an open grave singing the Service for the Dead for a woman of the people in an officially godless land.

When the Germans were at last in charge, people with some knowledge of events suspected that the Russians would be back, and now was the time to leave. A drinking party would be arranged somewhere along the shore, the German guards would be invited, and a fishing boat would slip in to pick up passengers on the way to Sweden. (Some of the people who came all the way to Canada in a sailing ship at the time ended their flight in Waterloo too.) Sweden was a safe haven for the rest of the war, and then my friends came to Canada. One evening I found them somewhat agitated. They had received an official letter from the Russians controlling Estonia, inviting them back with a guarantee of a safe welcome. They were fearful because the Russians obviously now knew where they had taken refuge, and might copy the manoeuvre of a boat drawing near the shore—say a Russian freighter on Lake Ontario—a quick abduction at night in an unmarked car, and a one-way ticket to a gulag or worse. But even if the Russians had long memories, they must have had other things on their minds than kidnapping a former state opera star and a former financial expert.

When Hella died from a heart attack there was a memorial programme for her on Estonian television (or radio) on which they played some of her recordings—all in spite of what must have been official disapproval. Her husband followed her in his time and it would seem that they left little trace in the community, but the marked rise in musical standards which I have seen in my time in Waterloo may owe something to them, as may also a local disinclination to look to the far Left as a cure for all our ills—but of that more later.

I must not leave the impression that Germans and Estonians were the only ones around the campus who still had ties with events in their lands of origin. For instance, the head of Romance languages once told me that his cousin was the girl to whom Michael Collins, the IRA leader, was engaged. And another faculty member told me that his relatives in Nova Scotia had maintained a safe house for IRA fighters who needed to be away from the action for awhile.

Before I leave the "campus mix" of Waterloo College, I should mention our Ojibway student who became fascinated by the story of Beowulf which, he said, resembled greatly the stories he had heard from his elders. He was lent a tape recorder from our equipment to take home over a holiday so that he could record some fragments that his father might remember, but he was defeated by the problem of translation. We may recall that Longfellow used a Finnish epic as a base for *his* adaptation of Indian legends, but I am not sure that *Hiawatha* was a successful recreation. (The Finnish language is close to the Estonian.) As an aside I might mention that my friend the opera singer believed there was a connection between some Amerindian languages and Estonian (and Finnish).

And our Canadian-born students had their exotic side too— exotic when compared to the norm on the campus. One of them, with a farming background, wrote notes to himself along the line of "Don't let them change you!" and he wore his farmer's braces in class, along with his workaday shirt and trousers. He later served as an effective teacher of literature in that strange hinterland where social gatherings involved recitations, and songs with new and original words, and step-dancing, all of which were featured at the party they gave him on his retirement. He is now helping a relative to farm and writes me that things have changed—no more teams of stalwart Clydesdales tramping up and down the fields, as he once had celebrated in a poem he wrote for our poetry magazine, but soulless high-tech machines about which it is difficult to wax poetic.

I could go on describing faculty, students, and friends of the college but I hope I have established the fact that we had on campus an atmosphere marked by diversity and equality, and not quite like that in any other academic milieu. In other words there was something in Waterloo College that was worth fighting to preserve when it became threatened by annihilation.

13

So far in the narrative I have hardly got myself on campus, but I can assure the reader that a couple of years after my arrival I was a part of the college family. We all worked hard since we offered pretty well the whole programme of the University of Western Ontario (i.e., general and honours), and Jim Clark and I were basically the English faculty. We had a complicated system of course rotation but would now and then have to give an extra section of something necessary for a handful of students to graduate. For instance, one year I taught Old English to one student who had managed to avoid it earlier in his career, and that was as much work for me as it would have been if I'd been teaching a class of twenty. (He came to enjoy the texts and would hold forth, expounding upon them to all who would listen in the Torque Room.)

The Torque Room has disappeared after years in its new location in the Central Teaching Building (Alvin Woods Building), and with it has gone some history. It was first a dining and coffee room in the basement of the new teaching and administration building (in 1954). Used by faculty, staff, and students, it became an intellectual as well as a social centre for all, a situation that inspired our bursar to name it the Torque Room (*torque* meaning the measure of a force producing an action). He had realized that a lot of action on campus came out of discussions and arguments prolonged over coffee in a congenial environment. It was congenial physically too. We were very happy with the "modern" conveniences and surroundings after the deficiencies of the old red brick *omnium gatherum* where we had operated before.

The student body increased steadily and with it our financial resources, although we were never comfortably well off and our salaries were lower than they would have been at a bigger institution. What made it all worthwhile was the quality of the students we attracted. Our proximity to them made it possible for us to feel their response to our efforts so that we taught to their needs while striving to have them leave us equal in training and information to anyone else from a university, even the University of Toronto.

Personally I found my life rewarding and pleasant. In 1950 I had joined a group called the Overseas Education League which was being taken to Britain by a Major Ney (father of a famous mayor of Nanaimo), a British military gent of the old style who felt Canadian educators should be exposed to the influences of the mother country. I can always date the great Winnipeg flood because I was able to take the place of a group member whose house had been inundated and required her undivided attention for the summer.

It was a sort of homecoming to land in Liverpool where I stayed with a friend in her home in a suburb called Waterloo, from which we made long excursions by bus (coach) to Wordsworth country. Then a trip through Housman country brought us to London, with side trips and events such as having tea on the terrace of the House of Commons with an MP, in this case a Sir David Robertson who represented the riding from which some of my ancestors had come to Manitoba in 1813–15. He pointed out that I was very lucky that my people had emigrated, which I interpreted to mean that prospects were not so good for young people in the northeast in 1950.

A trip to Paris took us through battlefields (the war was only five years in the past) and not far from the Canadian war memorial for 1914–18 which was a reminder of the suffering in both great conflicts. Paris, having been peacefully occupied by the Germans for so long, was flourishing. The big stores reminded me of Eaton's in Winnipeg, stocks were good (I bought gloves), and the Metro was clean and easy to travel. One evening a festive crowd near the Eiffel Tower reminded me of France's colonial history as I watched men in all varieties of uniform, and women in the dress of French possessions from Africa to Indo-China, enjoying themselves on a fine summer evening. The people at the hotel near the Gare du Nord were a bit supercilious. When I inquired about getting to a play (could it have been by Jean Anouilh?), I heard the hotel receptionist say to her companion, "*They* think *they* can understand it when even *we* cannot." My French wasn't good enough for me to tell her that trying to understand the theatre of the absurd happened to be my business. Perhaps that was why next summer I went to Laval—but more of that later. I did see a dreadful *Tristan* in Paris, but being in the famous Paris Opera House made up for it.

We ended our tour with a stay at the Edinburgh Festival, though I had also managed to visit friends in Cornwall and Hayward's Heath (I left my luggage at the place in Victoria Station, Brighton Line, where Miss Prism in the *Importance of Being Earnest* had deposited her handbag.) I left Edinburgh for a couple of days to go north as far as the little seaport from which some of my ancestors came—where I was given such a welcome by remote cousins that I had to stay an extra day. I saw Sir Thomas Beecham conduct, and enjoyed the original version of *Le bourgeois gentilhomme* when I got back to Edinburgh.

I have given the above details to indicate how much I would be able to enrich my classes on my return to Waterloo.

Earlier in this narrative I joked about the dress problems I faced when I came to Waterloo. I can close the subject once and for all by reporting that with our favourable rate of exchange I bought most of my clothes in Britain from then on, through Laura Ashley and Mary Quant until the time when one of my nieces grew up, moved to New York, and started sending me her castoffs to wear. The present motto, "You can wear anything you like," offers a more comfortable prospect than that presented to me on my arrival in Waterloo when everyone bought her suits at Kabel's and her dresses at Magda Lang's twice yearly sales. (The millionaires shopped in New York I was told.) Even though a somewhat feline graduate assured me once that a visitor to the campus had asked if I was a cleaning lady, I lived with myself quite easily, at least sartorially.

It has to be said that Britain in 1950 was still enduring rationing, so I hoarded my sugar and tea coupons to present to my hostesses when I visited the homes of friends. There were still plenty of bombsites that had not yet been cleared away, which were now overgrown with weeds. People seemed to be still exhausted after the long strain which at the end was heightened by the unmanned v2s which seemed more threatening than bombs dropped by real people. Eleven years later I went back to the Liverpool area where I had spent my first days in England and found a different country. The sunken-cheeked, work-stained faces on the buses had disappeared, thanks to dental care, health care, and better facilities for personal cleanliness in the new housing estates. In front of some houses men were proudly washing their new cars. Whatever happened later to dim the dream, Britain for a time was a brave new world.

In 1951 I tried to repair the deterioration in my French by enrolling in the Laval summer school. It was not my first visit to the province of Quebec; during the war I had spent a summer in Montreal, but that city, especially in wartime, was a distinct society in itself, and I felt that I wanted to get closer to the French fact. As a result I now find myself at a loss when trying to persuade intelligent and informed people in ROC (the Rest of Canada) that Quebec really is different. A tourist's eye view is not enough to give them the flavour of a world built to a degree on other assumptions than those subsuming British Columbia, for instance, and with all the variety there is in Quebec there is a homogeneity that may have changed somewhat since 1951 but which I believe still exists.

In Montreal, I lived in a room rented from a French widow who was looking after the family apartment while the other residents were the guests of a French industrialist living in Canada on some mission that had to do with materials of war. The apartment at the corner of City Councillors and Sherbrooke was right out of *La Bohème*. When someone rang downstairs, Madame opened the shutters, put her head out, and, assured that there was no danger, she pulled a cord that lifted the latch below so the delivery boy, or other visitor, could enter.

I said she was French, but she was really a Savoyarde from Nice. She had been a *dame de compagnie* she said, by which she meant a sort of temporary "woman Friday" for the noble and rich Europeans who spent the winters there. She told me she preferred the Russian aristocrats who had no airs and were generous. I thought of Mrs. Aksim. (A footnote here: my Estonian opera singer told me she once asked a colleague—a lively lady, I gathered—which lovers she preferred. The colleague replied, "Ah! the Russians. So romantic.)

My widow from Savoy had not forgotten her history. She talked of the counter-reformation massacre of her ancestors as if it had happened yesterday (making Milton's sonnet on the event much more immediate for me), and she detested the English, especially the royal family, whom she contrasted to Italian royalty whose ancestors had once ruled Savoy.

When the First World War was over, there were no men to whom she might marry her daughters so she came to Canada. She arrived on a dark, wet day—from sunny Nice—and swore to herself, she told me, "Never will I learn the language of this accursed country" (meaning English), which may have caused inconveniences for her, but was very handy for me because she regarded me as a good audience and I had to sharpen up my language skills in short order. I learned a lot that summer of 1942. Young women from all over Canada were working in munitions and there were just as many or more young men in uniform. But I didn't learn much about French-Canadians, whom Madame despised almost as much as the English.

I heard something of local musical gossip because her grandson, who soon returned to the apartment, played the viola in the symphony. I learned for instance that there was a move to get rid of the conductor because he was "un Belge," not even a Frenchman, and the players wanted a French Canadian. So you see, the distrust of English and ethnics revealed in Jacques Parizeau's post-referendum speech did not begin in 1995. A friend of my sister, a Greek with dark hair and skin, landed in hospital the day the news arrived of the loss about the Canadian soldiers in the Dieppe raid. She reported that some seminarians had gone on a rampage to attack any Jews or people they met who might be Jews, to punish them for sending French-Canadians to their death. Yes, I was shocked too, but not entirely surprised. I knew about Dreyfuss.

My Quebec adventure brought me into the middle of the real French Canada—at least in some of its aspects. The English fact was represented by the Chateau Frontenac where men and women actually danced together—something not allowed inside the city, hence the roadhouses in all directions of the periphery. (I didn't go bathing but if I had I would have seen both men and women decently covered. No bathing trunks allowed.)

I should stop to explain that my informant was again a widow, my French-Canadian landlady. She was a loyal daughter of the Catholic Church and of the province, but even she saw some contradictions in the life around her. She would explain some slightly deviant remark by the admission that her grandmother had been a Huguenot. According to the little history I remembered, that seemed impossible. There had been a thorough purging of heresy in the colony after an initial period of tolerance—but there she was, living proof that the books could be wrong. I also had believed that after the Plains of Abraham, etc., the seigneurial families had all left for France, yet Madame introduced me to a man, a French-Canadian, whose name I recognized as that of one of the old land-holding families.

Maurice Duplessis still ruled. I didn't go to one of his meetings but those who did told me the company chatted and laughed in their private conversations while he spoke, but he still could be feared. Madame quite approved of him.

The Church was everywhere. I met many fine, upstanding, intelligent, educated young men—all of them priests. I met mothers who were so happy that their sons had joined the priesthood. As a pragmatic bystander I thought it was a fatal waste of what would now be called good DNA (though we didn't know the term then). *Frère Untel*—that explosive little book which caused people to look again at the emperor's clothes—had not yet been written. (In Austria years later, I met a friend of Jean-Paul Desbiens, *Frère Untel*'s author, who told me he was punished for writing the book by being sent up to minister to the Eskimos, as we called them then.)

In the summer the city was flooded with members of teaching orders from all over Canada and the USA improving their qualifications. In the morning the buses and streets were brightened by nuns in habits of all colours and variations (Vatican II was still to come). As I walked to my classes in the old Laval, beyond the seminary I passed the chapel where perpetual prayer was offered for the canonization of Bishop Laval. In one of my classes dealing with Pascal, the priest or brother who taught us reminded us that the book of the *Pensées* was, or had been, on the Index. He seemed to be apologizing for talking about it in public.

It must have been on the eve of Saint Anne's day, July 26, that a great many of the young students at the summer school spent the night walking to Saint Anne. I heard them talking the next day of the exaltation they had felt on the pilgrimage. I myself went one evening to see a votive church, down in the Old Port, I think. It seemed to be built on water. Inside were suspended little models of boats and ships that had been saved by the intervention of Mary Protectress. (Perhaps this an example of the Stella Maria cult found especially among Acadians.)

One day Cardinal Roy came to greet the summer school students. I admit that I did not kiss his ring as did almost all the other students, but I admired him: handsome, tall, *sympathetique* (which is not quite the same in English). In our conversation group the chat came around to my surname, which is usually assumed to imply royalty. When I explained that it was instead a variant of *ruadh* (meaning red, red-haired), a clever nun who was our tutor that day pointed out that it was also possibly a variant of *roux* which may have come from the same Celtic root. Here was something to bind French Canadians and the others, an awareness of the similarities rather than the differences in our languages.

My landlady was conscious of a link with anglophones who were interested in culture. She was an admirer of Archdeacon Scott, the pleasant old-fashioned poet who by my time was supplanted in

"Canlit" classes by his son. She told me with approval of his funeral procession in which his medals (CMG, DSO) were carried on cushions.

I had gone to the little Anglican cathedral, of course, and wandered in the burial ground, noting the gravestones, one of a young wife buried there very soon after the conquest. (On one of my last visits I was unable to find it. Could it have become the parking lot I *did* find?)

My landlady belonged to the fringe of the upper class in Quebec, the fringe because her husband had died early and left her without means. Thus in meeting her friends, I was brought into contact with well-educated, charming men and women who were not likely to resemble the majority of citizens who lived in the lower town and round about the city, and whose loves and quarrels were being recorded by a young writer who came to one of our student picnics. I don't think his characters were yet on the radio as the Plouffe family.

As for the country folk, Maria Chapdelaine was long gone, though we read the book in one of our classes. My landlady told me that rural life changed when the mail-order catalogues began to arrive. (There was at least one good French-Canadian mail-order house in Montreal as well as, I expect, Simpson's and Eaton's.) Homespun gave way to smart synthetics and differences between social groups grew smaller.

What has all this to do with Waterloo College? As usual I brought my new insights to my classes, especially to my lectures on Canadian Literature. At least one of our honours students decided to go on to Laval for graduate work, partly inspired by my enthusiasm for a culture that an anglais might share before it disappeared. The province today seems very different from what I knew in 1951. Dr. Overgaard from our School of Business had something to do with the changes because he worked hard to raise standards in university business and economics departments, with particular attention to the province of Quebec where the need was greatest. This is no place to tell of the quiet revolution that seems to have eliminated most of what I have been describing. Yet, the world of 1951 is, as the colloquial phrase has it, the place where the Quebec of today was coming from. In 1951, however sophisticated and skeptical, however crude and superstitious individuals could be, practically a whole society lived its surface life with a steady undercurrent of what I can only call poetry: the family rosary, the hymns to the Star of the Sea, the constant reminder, often in gory and grotesque forms, of the Crucifixion. I am not sure what the undercurrent is now, but it may be that the symbols of nationhood are part of it.

This may be a moment for a brief appeal to bring imagination back into the sharing of our various Canadian heritages. As a child I thrilled to stories of Madeleine de Verchères and Adam Daulac, regarding them as part of my own past. Studies of constitutional conferences don't have the same affect. Why don't we share each other's novels or plays or films as we used to do? Part of the answer lies in our greater awareness of colonialism. Praising little Madeleine would mean showing the Indians against whom she and her brothers defended the fort in a not too favourable light, and we've become more sensitive about the other side of the story. At least in my classes I tried to bring together works of the imagination from both of our two solitudes.

Somewhere in my first years at the college, I also managed a quick trip to New York around New Year's. I spent a very few days rushing from ballet to theatre to cinema—and looking at the city. After a number of later visits, one of them at the height of the "burn, baby, burn" excitement, I find it hard to bring back to mind the New York of the late 1940s and early '50s. I joined a friend there but went around largely on my own, without any thought of danger. There was a magic in the lights in the tall buildings in the dark, wet winter days, with people selling violets on the street for women to pin on their fur coats. I don't think I met anyone who did not have a foreign accent, but I never felt threatened by their difference. I came back on a night train full of students sitting in dark coaches, studying for the half-term exams that were to come. The train stopped in the small hours at St. Thomas before it went on—to Chicago, I suppose. I cannot believe now that I got off into the snow without the slightest qualm—and, yes, there was a taxi there, just one, and the driver took me from St. Thomas to London to catch another train that got me to Kitchener in time to meet my first class of the day. Travel was easier then.

As I look back, I seem to have described a lot of gallivanting. My excuses are that, first, it was a relaxation after the long strain of graduate work, and the greater strains of working into a new academic position. In addition, my first year at the college, and in the Twin Cities, had shown me that it is very easy to become complacent with very modest achievements. It had been obvious that some people believed that what *had* been attained by college or city was enough for any reasonable being, and that pushing for more was a sign of pretension. All this was very bad for students who would have to make their way in a larger world. Our travels—ours, I say, because Jim Clark and his wife kept closely in touch with the New York drama scene, etc.—kept our students aware of new developments in the arts. Also, we were creating networks that would help them to go on to graduate work in places far from Waterloo County.

14

BEFORE I BEGIN ANOTHER SECTION of my recollections of life at Waterloo College, I should explain that the academic year then was somewhat shorter than it is now, and that attendance on campus during the summer holiday was not expected of faculty unless they were involved, as some were, in preparing for registration or doing other administrative tasks. That does not mean that one forgot one's courses and students, but it was possible to do other things. Like almost all younger academics in the late 1940s and early '50s, I always had my dissertation on my mind, but I didn't get much done on it because I needed a long stretch of time in which to read and think before pulling my ideas together. I decided to take off a year to do just that, living in Toronto in the University College Women's residence where I was a don. All of that is quite another story, but I can stop to say that at that time I discovered that I was never going to be able to enter into the mind of one member of my committee— a very nice man, a respected scholar, a "caring" person—and that, until he went on a sabbatical leave so that another professor could take his place, I should just mark time, in the interval, doing as much work on my own as I could. Luck was with me at the end of the 1950s: I handed in my thesis, had the oral, and was home free. I had enough sense of the academic realities to pursue that path, though my plan may seem a little unethical or even academically suspect, but I had seen enough students blocked by simple oppositions of personalities or approaches to make me determined not to let it happen to me. This is the first time I have confessed to my ruse; I felt I had to keep quite silent even after it succeeded.

There were alternatives to travel or study during holidays. We were closely involved in the extension programme of the University of Western Ontario, one of the most ambitious in the province, if not in Canada. I don't count extension departments that just worked on courses for the interest of mothers, farmers, or gardeners, etc. Western's courses were for academic credit, they were equal to those given to internal students, and they were everywhere. One of our feeble jokes was that if a man arrived on the moon, Western would start an extension course there. Waterloo College faculty were trusted to give full measure, and so were in demand. I myself gave courses in two summer schools in London, and one summer course for the University of Toronto in Toronto.

During the winter, each of us at Waterloo gave one or two courses for Western. I didn't have a car until late in the 1950s so I wasn't driving all over the province at night or on Saturdays, but I did get to Guelph on the bus year after year on the weekend, and I had a course in Galt at night at the old high school that involved a cold wait in the snow at the railway bridge for the CPR bus which would bring passengers back to Kitchener, I hoped in time to catch the last trolley bus home. Even when I was on leave in Toronto I succumbed to Angela's pleading (Angela arranged the extension programme) and gave a course in Brantford on Saturday mornings. One of my trips there coincided with Hurricane Hazel. While I waited for a bus to take me to the station, my boots filled with rain, but I was fortunate enough to catch the last train that left in the direction of Brantford. I don't think I had many students from a distance that weekend.

Towards the end of the 1950s my parents, who lived in Saskatchewan, suffered from increasing ill health, and my summers were given over to helping them as much as possible, though I tried to proceed with my dissertation when I could be at my desk in Waterloo. They died in the summer of 1959, which preceded the struggle that ended in the separation of Waterloo College from its offspring, the University of Waterloo.

Though the actual teaching terms seem to have been shorter than they are now, I believe that students and faculty in the 1950s were able to crowd in more extracurricular activity than is available to our present students. I must say in explanation that very few students were then working throughout the term to support themselves. That meant more time for reading and study—and for non-credit interests such as choir, drama, poetry magazine, etc. When I first came to the college, the students produced an original musical each year (the Purple and Gold), as did Western (Purple and White) and I believe a number of other universities. A student musical from McGill was presented in Stratford one year, I recall. Merely hanging around and avoiding classes in favour of writing or performing in the current musical was not officially encouraged, but it was said that a talented student-director at Western became a sort of perpetual student. I do not recall anything epoch-making in the Waterloo College productions, but they were acceptably entertaining. One tradition was to have a kick line, made up of football players or equivalents, which was always a hit.

Drama was very important in Lutheran congregations. When I first came here, members of the faculty were supposed to act as adjudicators in a drama festival where various young people's groups vied for top place. I rather think the activity operated like a hockey league with final play-offs. The standard of directing and acting was high, and competition was strong, sometimes even fierce. I had an unfortunate experience as an adjudicator when, having weighed all elements carefully, I ruled against an ambitious group. Their adult leader told me he would make sure I was never invited to judge plays again, and I was shunned as I left to try to find some way of getting home on my own (I think I may have walked). Some of our students participated in these festivals as members of their home parish groups, or as belonging to drama circles in local city parishes. I recall a production of *Riders to the Sea* which in technique and emotional impact equalled anything I might have seen in Dublin.

The head of Romance languages, Dorlyn Evans, was a Canadian who had been a liaison officer between Canadian and French troops in World War I. He produced and directed French plays on campus, drawing on his experience of the Comédie Française. Our French students would appear in costumes of the ancien régime, and perform stately minuets—a far cry from the kickline of the Purple and Gold shows. Incidentally, the director once told me something about administration that I have never forgotten: "There is never enough power to go around." It is as true of a university as of the court of a French monarch. He was a wise man.

Each spring the college choir led by Dr. Leupold (DMus, Berlin) would tour from parish to parish, giving concerts that reminded Lutherans of their college, and probably inspiring future students as well as present activities on campus too. At meetings of the gramophone club there were discussions of music and of performances. I believe it was at one of those that I saw Dr. Leupold sing an opera, accompanying himself at the piano. He was a match for Anna Russell. I don't recall the opera, but it may have been a parody of Wagner. At a Christmastime dinner given to the faculty by the board of governors, he was called on for a speech. He picked up his paper table napkin that depicted Santa and reindeer with parcels falling off the overloaded sleigh, and pretended to preach a sermon with the napkin as text—hilarious but perhaps not entirely enjoyed by the clergy present who may have recalled sermons of their own which kept a little too boringly to the words of a text. Of course, he too was a Lutheran pastor and was accepting his share of the teasing that he was extending to his brothers. I think his influence helped our students to realize that you can be funny without being superficial, and serious without being dull. The indigenous humour I found among people from country parishes when I first arrived dealt with topics like baldness, increasing waistlines, and other physical imperfections, but by 1960 the climate of the comic on campus has become more subtle and ironic. I should add that one of my first orders at our library was for a college subscription to the old *New Yorker* which may have had something to do with the change.

I recall a group of students from various levels gathering in my office during one academic year to read aloud and discuss their poetry. One of them whose girlfriend's father had access to a supply of suitable paper suggested that we publish a collection of student writing which we called *Chiaroscuro*. He left us at the end of the year to join his girlfriend at the University of Toronto, but the magazine carried on for a number of years under various editors. (An early contributor, John Robert Columbo, has had a distinguished career in Canadian letters.) *Chiaroscuro* may have been born shortly after we became independent—I cannot recall exactly—but I know that another little booklet, *Black Walnut*, featuring a collection of poems of an individual student in each yearly issue, was a product of the later WLU and went on for several years. O happy time before cutbacks. There was cash available for ventures of that kind.

We all seem to have entertained at home more than we do now. We would have student groups meeting at our houses or apartments, and a sort of family situation developed out of the encounters. Each year some faculty victim had to be advisor to the *College Cord*, the student newspaper. Some of our gatherings to discuss the forthcoming edition would be peaceful, but sometimes the advisor was caught between his/her aversion to censorship and his/her awareness of how the board of governors might view a certain article or headline. I was unlucky enough to be advisor in the reign of an editor who later was said to have demonstrated in Red Square against some Soviet shortcoming. (He seems to have gone unharmed.) I recall that almost every issue of the *Cord* raised problems in his tenure of office.

Students seem to be much less confrontational in 2004—they are more worried about the future, most of them have jobs to help pay the bills, and they may have ceased to believe that they can change things. By contrast, when I first came to Waterloo I inherited a group who had participated in the famous strike at Kitchener Collegiate. I don't remember what the issue was, but it brought the students out on the front lawn with placards and speeches and the school band, and the principal had to give in.

That lot resented any suggestion of control from above. For instance, when we suggested a visit to an art gallery, perhaps in Toronto, they said suspiciously, "Not in a bus that *you* hire." One of them left us to write the Great Canadian Novel in Paris, which he did, I have heard, on the walls of his dwelling. He corresponded with Ezra Pound in St. Elizabeth's Hospital until Pound took umbrage at the mention of a writer of whom he disapproved.

Life on campus can be enriched for faculty by the daily communication with colleagues, and Waterloo College was small enough to throw us in one another's way for an interchange of gossip, jokes, or opinions on all subjects. When the new teaching building made an office available for me on the second floor, opposite the biology lab, I never lacked for company.

The bursar, Edward (Ned) Cleghorn, father of our past university chancellor, was really a painter from Montreal who had sensibly learned business skills by which he could make a living. Before he returned to Montreal to be a curator at the Museum of Fine Art, his quiet humour and general "unflappability" helped me over some difficult times.

The head of Biology, who was from one of those Irish-derived communities near London, Ontario, was another warm-hearted, amusing raconteur, who kept me entertained with stories of life in his version of rural Ontario. For instance, he told of the last days of a female relative of his, aged ninety-nine years. The members of the family gathered to bid her farewell, but though the end was certain, it was delayed. To while away the time of waiting, the assembled family sang—and sang—with an occasional interruption as the old lady railed against the Lord for not granting her "her hundred." These were Protestants; I'm not sure that anyone has really depicted their lives properly in history or fiction, though there have been books about their Catholic counterparts, and by this time there must be few who remember.

Towards the time of the "split," more scientists were added to our faculty, and some of them mistrusted those of us in arts. One day when I was lecturing on T.H. Huxley, and opening up the problems arising out of his championship of Darwin, I told the class that I would never sign my name to a statement that I *believed* the Darwinian theory of evolution. Almost at once I had scientists standing around my desk urging me to recant! They didn't seem to realize that I was trying to have students see that a theory is a theory however well it is argued and supported, and that one must be prepared to change one's theories if other evidence should appear. This was my approach in almost all my university teaching: give students the evidence, that is the texts, and the bare facts regarding their generation, and then let the readers make up their own minds.

But I am afraid that I may have helped to increase the suspicions that the science side cultivated, suspicions that an arts faculty, and especially one in a church-related college would not do justice to their world view and their ideology, and that they would do better if separated from us.

15

WHEN I STARTED THIS ACCOUNT OF MY RECOLLECTIONS, I decided to leave out references to the weaknesses of the flesh in students, support staff, and faculty, unless certain incidents were so comic or tragic or significant for our history that they begged to be left in. However, since no story nowadays is complete without its quota of sex and violence, I am including a general discussion of both topics without going into personalities.

Such violence as there was in our tiny population on a small campus was generally excused as student pranks, though today some of those pranks would probably not be considered very amusing. For instance, it was possible to steal the clothes of someone in the showers in the old red brick building, and lock the door so that his only exit was onto the fire escape, where he would have to travel naked in full view of passersby until he regained his room in the dormitory. Since "streaking" had not yet become a form of attention getting, this manoeuvre caused considerable distress to the shy young men who tended to be its victims. I recall one young German immigrant who went into something like a breakdown (temporary, I think) after one such experience. Another young faculty member who was living in the men's residence area before his marriage was reading the newspaper one evening when a passerby casually ignited the paper at a lower corner without the reader being aware until later. Fortunately there were no fatal or even serious consequences.

There is a popular photo of students on the roof of the red brick building pouring pails of water down on an unsuspecting group, carefully arranged below for a photograph. When the students of the new associate faculty arrived on campus, they were targets for eggs hurled from the same roof, I am told. I have even heard that some of their faculty members received direct hits.

People used to call the new associate faculty "plumbers" because of their studies in technology. The "plumbers" in their turn seem to have despised the male students of the college, considering them to be seminarians or worse. (Many of our students at that time were preparing to enter the pastorate or school teaching and were therefore considered weaklings.) On one occasion the engineering students mounted a raid on the residence, which meant that they had to climb the stairway to the dormitory area. At the top stood several seminarians or teachers, one of whom was Mr. Ontario, ready to throw the plumbers back down the stairs. I heard that the raiders complained to our dean about the rough treatment they received, but I don't think the defenders were severely reprimanded. Mr. Ontario, by the way, had been the winner in a body-building competition.

The "plumbers" didn't stop to think that their antagonists came mostly from rural parishes or from small towns where recreation could be much more aggressive and even dangerous than in the cities. One of our students from such an area told me of how he and his friends had set oil drums on fire on a bridge that joined two parts of their town and had then stood behind the fires and taunted the police who were helpless on the other side.

One so-called prank on campus had to do with kidnapping the night watchman and wrapping his arms around the flagpole that used to stand in front of the old red building, securing his wrists with the handcuffs that he was foolish enough to carry as part of his equipment. The perpetrators were apparently on their way home from something like the old Waterloo Hotel and the watchman may have challenged them.

The Waterloo Hotel! Generations of students recall rowdy nights in the downstairs bar. A new proprietor tried to reduce casualties by serving beer in plastic glasses, but the move was not very popular. In today's version of the college, high jinks are, to a degree, kept on campus where drinking places are in the Student Union Building, but at the near-riot on Ezra Avenue at an end-of-term party in 1995, university authorities learned that the instinct for violence is not dead. (There were forty-two arrests, nine criminal charges, and a number of life-threatening injuries.)

Just after the "split" was made official, the interim president came into one of my classes looking somewhat distressed. He asked for two male students who, as usual, were not in class. In the corridor he told me the police were in his office looking for a couple who had heaved rocks through the windows of a filling station to emphasize their displeasure with the management. I did not follow the case, but some threatening telephone calls that had been annoying the English faculty ceased about this time, from which I conjectured that the culprits had been those in the former offence and that they had somehow been removed from our midst.

I also recall a vague story of a female student being carried off into the men's residence and deposited in her boyfriend's room, which seems to have been a symbolic gesture since mingling of the two main sexes in residence rooms was forbidden in Waterloo College. She was not a great weight to carry, and she was a good sport, albeit without the reputation of being "fast," and so the whole event was regarded as a great joke, not a sexual assault. Several years ago an unthinking don in one of our men's residences suggested to some of his charges that they might revive the old custom of "panty raids" which had enlivened the 1960s and '70s. The raid occurred, a feminist professor informed the press, and WLU was denounced on the radio. After a campus committee was convened to investigate the affair, penalties were imposed and the new proprieties were observed, though some of the young women involved were reported to have complained about "old biddies interfering in their fun." It is difficult to be categorical about sex on campus in any era. The fact that men and women were not allowed to be together in residence rooms in college days, and the contrasting fact that now such visiting is allowed, though with posters in washrooms saying "Report date rape," might suggest a great alteration since 1950, but my impression is that actual practice hasn't altered a lot though the language has changed a very great deal.

Not long ago I heard a youngish speaker on the radio holding forth on the subject of the sexual revolution, which she seemed to think had happened sometime around 1968. It was clear she didn't know, for instance, that contraception was almost as old as time, and that condoms, now an essential component of romance, have had a long history, though modern chemistry has improved on lamb skin.

Now I have a chance to ride a hobbyhorse of mine for a few minutes. I have long had the belief that the sexual revolution really took place around 1739, in anglophone countries at least, with the inauguration of Dr. Coram's Foundling Hospital in London, and grew with the movement, labelled as "sentimental," that cultivated pity for the unfortunate, especially unwanted babies, but including women—who had for almost all time been victims, not only in love but in all the material transactions of life. The new attitudes included an awareness of responsibility for women's welfare, such as we find later in John Stuart Mill, along with demands for freedom and equality such as those voiced earlier by Mary Wollstonecraft. The result was what became Victorianism, which can be regarded as anti-sexual and repressive insofar as it put *woman* on a pedestal and imprisoned her as "the angel in the house," but looked at another way, the period may have fostered some acknowledgement of the responsibility involved in fathering illegitimate babies on poor young women, or imposing numerous pregnancies on wives. As movements do, Victorianism swung to an extreme of prudery, especially in an aspiring lower middle class, but by the 1920s, after the First World War, that swing back to more sexual freedom was obvious. I recall as a child observing a family cousin, a flapper whose relations with her young man (what *did* they call them then if they weren't fiancés?) didn't look very platonic. At the height of the latest sexual revolution, just before Rock Hudson died, bringing AIDS to the attention of the media, someone (it may have been Ken Tynan) said that anyone should be able to accost anyone he or she fancied, anywhere, at any time, and if both were willing, immediately copulate. But I recall that during the Second World War that happy day had almost arrived. If one ever had to go through a public park at any time, one had to pick one's way carefully in order not to step on happy couples, who had probably been acquainted only for the short time the young soldier had been stationed near that city.

Our students at Waterloo College had been around in the war years, and were quite aware of sexual liberation. Some were promiscuous. I recall hearing the comment, made elsewhere, that "sex was good exercise among friends." One young woman was very much on the mind of her former boyfriend (again, what was the term?) who still cared about her. She had left him to play the field. He told me the nuns at her school had impressed on her indelibly that contraception was wrong, but she seemed to have missed the class on promiscuity.

Most young women at the college seemed to regard "going all the way" as a sign of commitment. Whatever the intent of their intimacy, a lot of our college students found their future spouses on campus (students in nursing took some courses with us along with the regular students) and established connections that have lasted over forty years, as I am reminded by each year's Christmas greetings from former students and their families.

The big difference between sex in 1950 and in 2004 was, as I have said, in the language, but changes in law, technology, and in lifestyles have brought legal abortion, more types of contraception, more single mothers—more freedom, but I am not sure more happiness. And the economic downturns since the 1950s have made life more difficult for wives and mothers who must be good employees, good wives, *and* good mothers. *Plus ça change.*

I earlier mentioned that the two sexes were not allowed to be together in the dormitories, hinting that, of course, there could be no similar move against same-sex cohabitation. I cannot claim any great knowledge of the private lives of homosexual students any more than of heterosexuals, but the little I heard suggested that among male students there was considerable understanding of differences. I was told that a group of male students arranged a late-term visit to a cottage in the country where they shut up one of their number with a sympathetic guy who was actually a psychiatrist, and that after a very agitated night during which the victim rushed out several times screaming that he wouldn't put up with it, and was forced back to confront his self, he "came out of the closet" as a later era would come to express it, and has since lived what I gather has been a happy life. I know it has been successful.

I never heard of a lesbian relationship among our college girls. There were not many women in the student body, so the law of averages might not have applied. In the time just after independence, there was a female Don Juan in the women's residence who kept the atmosphere strained. I don't recall a novel that really conveys the trouble that kind of character can cause. Not only does she attract women and discard them at will, but she incites jealousy and quarrels on other bases than sex, seeming to enjoy the power.

Strangely enough, a relative of one of our administrators was so unwise as to marry one of these, a professional woman, whose attempts to get his money resulted in a court case reported in the newspapers. Among the interesting details was her report that her husband was impotent, and that she had bought an ocelot to keep him away from her.

But back to the subject: a friend who is a nun told me the lady Don Juan concerned had been appointed as a family physician to some of the sisters, and thus gained entrée to a convent. Though I don't think she persuaded anyone to break her vows, she succeeded in setting one against another in various ways, and created such a tense atmosphere that the more worldly wise members had to work hard to end her connection with the place and keep the members together.

I suppose men have the same gift for creating strife.

Flora Roy, Department of English, 1954. Jim Clark, associate professor of English, 1950s.

Aerial photo of campus, 1957.

Canadian Officers'
Training Corps, 1953–54.
Front row, L to R, Jim
Cotter, J.M. Clark, RSC,
Bill Marden; back row,
L to R, Dave Armstrong,
Jim Breithaupt, Bob
Binhammer, Gerry Holle.

Dr. Ulrich Leupold at the piano, 1940s. Elmer Iseler, standing on the left, became
one of Canada's best-known choral conductors and received an honorary degree
from the university.

J.G. Hagey, president of Waterloo
College and later the first president
of the University of Waterloo.

Dr. Herman Overgaard, professor of
economics, 1950s.

Dr. Herman Overgaard with an economics class, 1948-49.

Initiation Week, 1948. Erich Schultz, who became WLU's chief librarian, is fifth from left in back row. Photo: Harry Huehnergard, *The Record*.

Waterloo College Library, late 1940s; students preparing assignments.

Debating Club, 1954-55.

Student operating a Gestetner machine, c. early '50s.

Above and below, students "studying" in the men's dorm in the late '40s and early '50s.

The Cord Weekly, containing articles addressing the status of the College, October 23, 1959.

Students in a dormitory room in the late '60s.

The arts and science building, which opened in 1954.

College Faculty, 1952. Sitting, 2nd from left: James M. Clark, Rev. Lloyd H. Schaus, H.T. Lehman, last on row, Rev. George Durst; second row: 2nd from left: H.W. Wright, Helmut H. Binhammer, Mrs. M.E. Lewis, (skip one), Otto W. Heick, W. Dorland Evans; third row centre: Flora Roy.

Waterloo College, Willison Hall, late '50s. It was torn down in the late '60s.

Top: Waterloo College pact signing, 1956.
Bottom: first Board Joint Committee Meeting, February 22, 1957.

Flora Roy, 1988.

A 1973 aerial shot of the Wilfrid Laurier University campus, with Seagram Stadium.

PART TWO

Waterloo College Becomes
Waterloo Lutheran University

Aerial view of campus, 1957.

16

THE SUBJECT I HAVE BEEN AVOIDING all this while is not sex, but politics—politics in the wider sense of competing ideologies, or prejudices disguised as ideologies, all mixed up with self-interest and altruism and much else. Perhaps I have been avoiding it because I don't want to sort out my own political leanings, which are just as mixed up with illusions of status or errors in logic as are those of the people I shall try to describe. Here are some of the elements of campus life that started to open up cracks from about 1955 to the final splitting of a part of Waterloo College to become Waterloo Lutheran University.

First my own position as observer. I don't think anyone on campus knew what my political position was. A colleague once said to me, "you are an Anglican, and so you must be a Conservative." I just laughed, not confessing that the grandfather who had come from Ontario had a framed photograph of Laurier's first Cabinet on the wall of his kitchen, to which spot it had, I suspect, been banished by the women from the parlour with the horsehair sofa. I had for quite some time been a refugee from political affiliation, perhaps because I am a coward. I had learned early that politics is for real, and that if you enlist in any army you are bound by its rules, and if you are defeated or defect you are punished. (Perhaps I should have used the past tense since our former Liberal prime minister Jean Chretien once made former Conservative prime minister Kim Campbell an ambassador.)

I had grown up in a Progressive household. I use the capital P because there was a Progressive Party then, which was devoted to reform of the various shortcomings of Conservative or Liberal rule. When the Conservatives invited a Progressive premier of Manitoba to head their party, he insisted on joining the two names, whence the Progressive Conservatives. I recall attending an all-day political meeting of the party as a child, and there were Progressive evening gatherings at our house. In the meantime a movement that should properly be called Christian Socialism, though the enthusiasts I knew were proud unbelievers, was growing. I was interested in the principles they discussed, and attended many social gatherings of adherents who had wit, sociability, and intelligence. When the time came that one of the group asked me if I would stand for nomination as a federal candidate for the Cooperative Commonwealth Federation (CCF), I was very young (early twenties), bent on an academic career, and I must confess more interested in clothes, dancing, and boys than in dull meetings in community halls and school houses. I refused, and the woman who accepted was elected and went to Ottawa. (Gladys Strum was elected MP in 1945, and MLA in 1960 and 1964.) I have never regretted my decision though I found later that an academic life for a woman in those days was not easy and precluded less serious interests such as dancing. During the war I attended a conference at a camp on the west coast where I saw several members of the J.S. Woodsworth family, one of the founders of the CCF, among them the woman who had once confided to a friend of mine her sad fate as his political daughter. Later she had married a friend of her father's to become a political wife. I did not envy her though I respected her. Perhaps I am just a more selfish being. Also I'd had some proof of the political dangers one can walk into. At the time when I was being wooed by the CCF, Saskatchewan was run like a totalitarian state. The government of the day had an agent in each community who had a list of the local voters, and from that list he chose for all the government jobs in his purview only those who were dependable government supporters. (Among the agents I met was a godson of Louis Riel. He'd been delegated to run a Métis community.)

A couple of agents were overheard by one of my friends as they foolishly talked on a party line about the failure of a plot to have me dismissed from a job so that the daughter of one of them might replace me. I was actually leaving the job to go to university, but I was shaken to learn that the government's hand could reach into private lives to that extent. I did not want to fight or to surrender, so chose instead a detachment from all political action. And so I ended as a silent Christian Socialist who believed in private property. No wonder I was attracted to the study of the eighteenth-century where people who could have professed such contradictory views might be found. This all made me a detached observer somewhat like the eighteenth century Joseph Addison, though without his aristocratic connections. It also made me an enigma to the politically curious. If I avoided joining the Left, in spite of understanding their views, I would have been seen as living in bad faith. If I refused to move to the Right, though clinging to such property and privileges as I had, I would be "a commie in our midst." Much better to be silent, and when election day came, vote for the least repellent candidate and principles.

To relate my approach to politics to the actual events and undercurrents in Waterloo College, I must go back to 1948 when I arrived. Kitchener and Waterloo politics were a great mystery. The area managed a fine balance: when the representation in Ottawa was Conservative, that of Queen's Park was Liberal, and vice versa. And when the federal member was Liberal, there was apt to be secret dealing with the opposition, as my landlady inadvertently revealed when she reported that local leaders had just had a quiet meeting with George Drew which she begged me to forget. (George Drew had been the Progressive Conservative premier of Ontario from 1943 to 1948.) I never knew the political preferences of the administrators of the college, though I suspected that they were inclined to the Liberal Party.

What was sure was that anyone who was anyone here was not on the Left. In those days Left meant the Trades and Labour Council and those people who made things difficult for leaders of local industry. There was a rumour that in one of the local cemeteries there was a tombstone with a hammer and sickle engraved on it, and another later rumour that it had been erased, signs of an early attachment to Marxism and a repudiation by another generation. My life in the Twin Cities would not, however, bring me in touch with whatever remnants there were of a workers' party.

In 1948 it was not fashionable for academics to be "bolshie" (as the British later called it), but since no academic then admitted to being on the Right, it was generally assumed that most professors had some sympathy with the Left. What everyone seemed to be united on after 1950 was a determination not to let McCarthyism take hold in Canada. Canadian academics were closely in touch with American universities. Many were studying and writing dissertations in the USA, and knew first hand what the witch hunt was doing there to academic life and intellectual life in general. One of my friends who now admits to being pretty far right of centre told me that, when he was a student at Columbia, he refused to answer the question when asked if he was or had ever been a communist, just to show solidarity with other academics and with the principle of free speech.

To protect academic freedom in Canada, and to champion university faculty in general, the Canadian Association of University Teachers was founded in 1951, and at Waterloo College we formed a faculty association with similar aims. In my opinion, the CAUT has never had a serious case of violation of a faculty member's right to free speech such as we heard about from the USA, though it has been called on from time to time. As the political climate has shifted, its problems have become more complex. In our own time, how is a watchdog for free speech to regard the claim of the faculty member preaching pedophilia in Toronto, or the professor at Western who believes his research indicates that some races are more intelligent than others? In the 1950s the questions were more likely to be about open defences of Stalinism or attacks on religion, both of which were generally condoned by administrations, though in the face of protests from some members of the general public, such as letters from "Disgusted, Tunbridge Wells." Sorry, that is "Disgusted, Owen Sound." (Just kidding!) My weak joke indicates that at first we didn't take the matter of academic freedom too seriously.

How much communist influence was there in Canadian universities in the 1950s? I had met a few party members myself. A classmate at Saskatchewan, from a British labour family, had been a Young Communist, but had got out when she saw the control that was exerted on her from Moscow through the Canadian party. This element of control was apt to alienate the brighter members who would prefer to choose for themselves the causes they would foster or attack rather than following Moscow's orders blindly.

Carlyle King, an English professor at the University of Saskatchewan, told me that when he became active in the CCF in the province, one of his painful tasks was to purge the movement of Communist Party members who were pushing into it with, one assumes, the intention of taking it over—at least as long as Moscow wished. Some of them had been his students, and had probably been inspired by his enthusiasm for social justice, which for them at the time seemed to have been achieved in the Soviet Union and in China. (I recall some of my own nearest and dearest later putting photos of Stalin and Mao on the wall to be an inspiration.)

The war in Spain brought out more endorsement of the far Left in the pre-1939 intellectual world. Franco's Moorish battalions appalled the *bien pensant*, and the news of Canadian boys fallen in Spain evoked sympathy. As a student I was taken to visit a mother in Saskatoon who was waiting for some definite news of her son who was missing. She said that day after day, young men on their way home dropped in to give her what news they could. It was clear who were the good guys and the bad guys, in that war, at least until one read Orwell, or even Hemingway whose book about the war hinted at the horrors in the campaigns as Stalinist agents eliminated other Leftist parties.

I have already mentioned that ominous-looking young men filled up my lecture room when I was to speak on *For Whom the Bell Tolls*. One of my students (who may have been the one who had alerted the troops) told that he had "made up his mind," meaning I gathered, that he had joined the party. I knew, too, that one of the most pleasant graduate students in English at the time was a party member.

My own position? I'd never had as much confidence in the Soviet utopia as had my friends, even at the beginning of my study of modern history. During the Second World War we saw many films of the boy-girl-tractor genre depicting the happy Russian workers on the collective, but I was uneasily aware that the characters were actors, and after the war I became acquainted with a Ukrainian DP (Displaced Person) who told me of the Stalin-created famine that had killed peasants on an unprecedented scale. I learned too that Nikita Kruschev, whose rise seemed to betoken a change for the better after Stalin, had taken part in the grain collections that had set off the famine. My DP friend told me her mother was approached at the height of the hunger by a starving man who had earlier carried off her grain, now begging for a meal from the little amount she had managed to hide from him. My Estonian friends too had furthered my education on Stalinism, and when Tim Buck (head of the Communist Party in Canada) stood on a public platform and assured a questioner from the floor that stories of the forced evacuation and murder of Estonians were completely untrue, I decided that he was either dishonest or so blindly loyal to the party line that his mind could not take in an alternative. Either way he was not someone I could believe or respect, and I felt the same about his followers, though more of them came to have misgivings about the Moscow line after 1956 (i.e., after the Soviet invasion of Hungary) and dropped away from the party.

As far as the general Canadian public was concerned about Stalinism, I think there was considerable sympathy for our Russian allies who fought desperately once they had been told which side they were on. I met a young man in Montreal who had gone as a sailor on a freighter carrying supplies to Murmansk, but he did not profess any admiration for the Soviet system. His motivation was a wish to meet new girls. As he told the story (to considerable mirth at a party), he endured dive bombing, enemy fire, ice, and snow, to arrive and see the female stevedores who were lined up to unload the ship. They were big strong women doing what was considered men's work and they destroyed his fantasy of the waiting, "easy" Russian girls. All his visions of Russian floozies who would be a nice change from those waiting in western ports had led him through hell—and he had to get back the same way, which he did, safely.

When the war was over, the Russian tourist agency (Intourist) did considerable business guiding visitors in groups or singly to places where, in another version of Potemkin's fake villages, like-nesses of the idyllic collectives of the war-time films could be displayed. I wasn't one of the visitors though I did learn a little Russian, and I remained an admirer of the great nineteenth-century writers, and of some of the twentieth century. I showed admirable Soviet films to my world literature classes, and enjoyed Soviet music and ballet. But I still remained uneasy about getting closer to a power that I regarded as mysterious and unpredictable. Later, after the founding of WLU, I took a couple of trips on Russian ships. The first, in 1967, was in an atmosphere of suspicion, and of authority directed from above. The whole crew of the *Alexander Pushkin* were naval personnel, I was told, and passengers were under discipline too. A large firm woman stood in the dining room directing us to our places, and overseeing the harried young men who were our waiters. This authoritarianism extended everywhere. A young woman travelling to a German destination with her husband had a miscarriage. In the ship's hospital the doctors proceeded to "clean her up" (I think it was D and C) and when she begged for an anaesthetic they informed her that they didn't provide it in Russia for that procedure, and if she screamed they would tie her down to the table. Her husband was almost beside himself with rage but was soon quieted. I had told my friends that if I didn't show up in London on time they should go to Canada House to start inquiries, because not long before an innocent American professor had been seized in the street in Moscow and held hostage to be exchanged for a Russian being held by the Americans, and the same sort of thing could have happened to anyone on the boat. The second trip (in 1972 on the *Lermontov*) was after the defection of Stalin's daughter and the head of passenger recreation even made a sly joke about it, which was a sign that everything was becoming more relaxed. Even so I was not ready to believe that Soviet Russia was an earthly paradise. In time this was to put me at odds with new colleagues who had quite different ideas, and to force me in the end into the party that decided to stay with the Lutherans and their new university.

17

I HAVE INDICATED THAT ALTHOUGH THE CANADIAN academic world in the early 1950s was Leftish (with few protests from the Right, such as would become common by the late 1990s), there was little danger of our academia becoming communist, either of the Stalinist or Trotskyite kind, though there were sympathizers or "fellow travellers" on both sides. Yet underneath there was doubt. The revelations of Igor Gouzenko in 1945 about Soviet spying in Canada had not spawned a Canadian McCarthy era, but it was established that people in our midst had really been spying for a foreign power. This was reprehensible, even if that power had for the large part of the recent war been our ally.

Occasionally we still hear of renewed efforts by independent investigators to see the sealed files of the RCMP which would show, as it was put rather bluntly, "how the Mounties were spying on Canadians." Even after the opening of the KGB files, it is obvious there are trusting people who don't realize that some Canadians were involved in activities and affiliations that were at best questionable, and at worst treasonous, and about which it was best to be informed.

I expect that when the files are opened by name, I will be in there as an informant. Towards the end of the 1950s, one day I was shown into the dean's office to be very obviously left alone with a smooth young man (smooth hair, moustache, smile, suit) who said he was making some inquiries about a faculty family. The wife's brother, he said, had applied for a sensitive post, and the authorities wanted to know if he would be reliable. It was clear that this was a political vetting. I felt that the course nearest to honesty would be to state that I had no real knowledge of the political opinions of the couple concerned. If I had voiced my suspicions, I would have said that I myself would not put one of the family in an ultra-sensitive spot. I heard afterwards that a quite responsible student had declared that the faculty member we were discussing was communist, and

I had my own opinions of his reliability—but none of that is in the files, thank goodness, though it will be obvious that I did not whole-heartedly vouch for the family. Today, membership in any political party might seem of little consequence, but in those days such seemingly innocuous things were reported all the time.

By the middle of the 1950s a new breed of academic was arriving on university faculty rosters. They had come of age after the war and didn't seem to have taken in the ethical complexity of issues that my generation had to struggle with. For instance, as I have suggested, should one support a cruel authoritarian regime (the Soviet one) so long as it is fighting an equally repellent enemy (the Nazi one)? And that question had included all kinds of permutations and combinations in the Balkans and elsewhere. The world just after 1945 seemed much more simple, but it was not long before other injustices made claims on a rising generation of dissidents. My friends in Britain labelled them Bolshie. Primarily, younger academics were consciously trying to be different from the generation that had fought and managed the war. However, in universities there were plenty of genuine aggravations that *were* different from wartime concerns: the power of the administration, the entrenched academic approaches (especially in arts departments), and where there were church ties, there was sensitivity about anti-religious polemics.

At Waterloo College, the increased enrolments after the war brought to the campus enough of the new generation of academics to challenge the way we had been living with paradoxes. For instance, Darwinism existed uneasily with any sort of theological approach to development. Even if they were not questioned about it, the scientists of the faculty felt they might be. I've heard there was dismay in our science departments when I expressed reservations about a simple version of Darwin's theories. There was an open policy on hiring, but I believe that some candidates were questioned about their approach to Christianity. The dean was completely liberal: he once showed me a memo pad that was less than an inch wide which he kept on his desk. "For narrow-minded Lutherans," he said. The board of governors may not have been as broad-minded as we could have wished.

The Lutheran group with which the college was associated was just at the turning point. Soon the older, more conventional clergy would retire, and younger men (they *were* men in those days) would take over the board, and a theology that was aware of developments in science, in the social sciences, and in biblical scholarship would follow. I, for one, never heard an objection to anything I said in lecture or seminar, and I was prepared to wait for ideas to broaden as our graduates took over from their elders.

The new young faculty were not going to be as patient. In English, especially, there was another type of authority against which to rebel: I was a woman. One of the new men always addressed me as "Boss." Another informed me that, at a conference of academics in English he had just attended in the USA, a resolution had been passed declaring that the head of an English department should never be a woman. As I shall have occasion to repeat later, that opinion was also expressed by one of the most influential men in the new University of Waterloo. Here these Young Turks were, teaching courses prescribed by another authority figure at the University of Western Ontario, watched over by a board made up of Lutherans, and headed by a woman who didn't intend to allow deviation from the Western curriculum—after all, the honours papers were marked by the faculty who had set up the courses in London. No wonder my young colleagues felt frustrated. Tension was mounting.

The eruption came, not in Waterloo but in Winnipeg. Professor Harry S. Crowe had been dismissed from the faculty of United College. The CAUT intervened and he was reinstated, but left when some colleagues who had resigned in sympathy with him were not reappointed. As I heard it, the situation was a great deal more complicated. At the time I had a lot on my mind, chiefly the need to get my dissertation finished, and the greater need of my parents whose health was failing. Because I had connections with family and friends in Winnipeg, I was interested personally in addition to my concerns about academic freedom as a department head. My information was that Professor Crowe, who was off campus, wrote a private letter to a friend at United expressing his opinion of the administration and institution and probably of the United Church in what I gather was colourful detail. The friend inadvertently left it lying around. It was picked up by an unknown, read, and deposited on the principal's desk with a note attached, "How is this for loyalty?" (or words to that effect). The letter was so defamatory that the principal dismissed the author, and the fireworks began. My only problem with that story is that a friend of mine, visiting Brandon College, was shown a copy of the letter. If the whole situation was spontaneous, how did it happen that copies had got about? According to Victor Catano, the CAUT president, "the Harry Crowe case" was a seminal event in the history of CAUT." Harry Crowe had written about "the corrosive force of religion," which among other things, confirms his reputation as a troublemaker in 1958 (<www.caut.ca> October 2003 Bulletin).

A member of our faculty at WLU told me not long ago that he had been a student at the time, and that he had stuck with the college though he came from a family involved in workers' movements. (Winnipeg certainly had them. Remember the famous 1919 strike.) He had little regard for those of the Crowe party who had remained on the faculty. As he said, "Why would 'they' do this to United?" He went on to mention what I already knew—that in the past United had given refuge to a number of activists, writers, and thinkers who would have been too eccentric, too critical, and too expressive for most faculties at that time. It looked as though the generations were turning over. Crowe and friends were the new rebels, ready to take charge of an institution that they now saw as stuffy, stiff-necked, religious—in short, old-fashioned.

My family recollections of Winnipeg offered more insights. If Marx didn't say "follow the money," some other shrewd observer did—and money in Winnipeg that didn't come from the Grain Exchange came from real estate. United College was (and still is) sitting on some of the most valuable land in the city. The University of Manitoba was trying to persuade United to move out to its campus on the outskirts. At the time I didn't think the university was too unhappy about the troubles at United. Not only were there the differences about location but there was an impression that the college outranked the university in some areas. The university, after all, was a jumped-up agricultural college that had spent years trying to become academically respectable. I don't say that I approved of that view (both my parents had diplomas from the agricultural college) but there were other people in the family who had graduated from Manitoba College—one of the "united" parts of United—who would have agreed with it.

I am not hinting that a mysterious power (*they*) set out to destroy United, but I cannot overcome a suspicion that the president was "set up" in the Crowe case, and that there were bystanders who would not have minded if the college had been so blackened by the case that it would be unable to attract students and faculty, or at least lose its enviable reputation. In reality, though United limped along for a time, it eventually recovered to become the successful University of Winnipeg, still firmly seated on its valuable land.

A judiciary hearing, such as was held by the inquiry committee of the CAUT in the Crowe case, cannot deal with prejudices or suspicions. I am sure it decided rightly on the basis of the surface evidence. If Waterloo College, church-related, perhaps right of centre, with a growing reputation for academic excellence, fell into the same or a similar trap, what would be our fate? As it turned out, by the time there was a cry of "academic freedom" our situation had become so convoluted that only Solomon could have sorted it out, and indeed we came to a sort of Solomon's solution in the separation of the two universities.

18

BEFORE I BEGIN TO TRY TO CHART THE EVENTS that led to the division on our campus (a division which quickly turned into a gulf), I should say more about my own position. I cannot recall at which stage Murdo McKinnon of the English department at Western told me that they would look after me if it came to the worst, but even before that I had decided that I was not going to become a part of the new university. My strength was in literature and my place was in an institution with a strong arts faculty. As I viewed the new dispensation, it looked as though power would lie in the engineering area or in the pure sciences and mathematics, as future trials of strength would decide. I wasn't worried about employment. I could appeal to

Professor Woodhouse in Toronto if necessary and become one of those useful women who at one time were found on all campuses, filling in where necessary and making a tolerable living in pleasant surroundings. It would have been a step down from department head, but I'd be in Toronto, which had its excitements. I should miss the friends and associates of Waterloo College, but it was impossible that the easy relationship of faculty, students, and administration could last after the expansion that was planned. Thus, in the troubles of the late 1950s, I was able to care and not to care.

I had another advantage: for most of my life I had enjoyed a certain detachment from what went on around me as if it were art, partly as visual display, but also as it might appear in fiction. I especially enjoyed irony in many forms, and there was plenty of it in any human situation. Even in painful disagreements I found some entertainment, and once or twice in the last two years of the 1950s I burst into genuine laughter at the discovery of some otherwise shocking contradiction.

Of course, not all the battles we engaged in could be regarded as art forms. Against the most painful, my German doctor, much involved in our struggles because she was a Lutheran faculty wife, provided me with modern armour. I had a prescription for something, I knew not what, that made me sleep at night even after the most painful events of the day. It seemed cowardly to avoid the battle to that extent, but I was able to carry on and, I believe, to be a useful ally for the Lutheran party that wished to hold onto the college. Also, I was never hooked on her prescription.

So I deserve no sympathy. That should be saved for my colleagues who had families to support and academic reputations to sustain, and who took the risk of becoming unhireable if things turned out badly.

It started with the college's ambition to become free of the connection to Western and to expand. Into what? That was the question. The Association of Manufacturers, etc. had made a pronouncement. They did not want to hire young people just out of high school, but they were not particularly interested in the usual university graduates. They wanted employees who would not have to be completely trained on the job, and who were old enough to be responsible. What was envisaged was something like the community colleges that were later developed.

The head of Waterloo College's board of governors at the time was Gerald Hagey, a sales employee of the local branch of a rubber company. The official historians of the University of Waterloo, whose books I have not read, will have described his early career so I need to add only a few details. He was not only a graduate of the college, but had been a pupil in the college school for boys. Rumour had it that he put himself through college by playing poker. Later he was said to be able to sell anything to anyone. He was not universally admired, some say because of his persistence and ubiquity. He lived as hard as he worked. I always tried to avoid his kindly offers of a ride in his expensive car because he had some difficulty in keeping a license after many traffic violations.

There may be a record of his conversations with local industrial leaders before plans for expansion of the college were put forward. All I know is that Gerald Hagey became president of the college, a degree was found for him from an American Lutheran university, and he became Dr. Hagey. A friend who was registrar, and I believe at one point dean of the College of Optometry in Toronto, recalls an unadvertised visit to see President Hagey in his office in our old teaching and administration building where they discussed possible affiliation of the Toronto college to the new entity that was evolving in Waterloo. This, he says, was quite early in the 1950s. What I recall is a proposal to found a satellite faculty that would deal with practical training, and could receive government money that would not be available to a church-related establishment.

The example of McMaster was cited. It had begun such an enterprise with much success. I don't think anyone pointed out that the Baptists had then given up their university. I wonder if the participants in the very early discussions about the future venture into academic planning were aware that the Lutherans would lose theirs. Taking over an existing organization and turning it into something else was not unusual in either academe or in industry. A friend in England told me of the excellent little engineering college where he had worked which was turned into a complete university without its original base.

The records tell us that "in 1956 a non-denominational board was established to obtain government grants to run expanded science programs under the name Waterloo College Associated Faculties. The Associated Faculties began operation in 1957.... In 1959... the provincial government established three universities—the University of Waterloo, the University of St. Jerome's College, and Waterloo Lutheran University College which along with the Seminary made up Waterloo Lutheran University" (from *WLU Support Staff, 1911–1986,* 75th anniversary pamphlet). The dates and straightforward statements make the story look plain, but the events between 1956 and 1961 were something other than simple.

The intention at first seems to have been to create something like a community college that would be more than a trade school. As discussion raised the target, talk was of a Canadian MIT or California Tech. Little Lutheran Waterloo College was becoming redundant in the plan. What to do? When we looked at Toronto we found church-related colleges gathered under the wing of the university. Could we bring in St. Jerome's and perhaps other denominations in something less than a federation, with the university in control more than in Toronto? (The scaling back of Toronto's church colleges was far in the future.) The telephone call I mentioned early in my narrative, jubilantly proclaiming that Anglicans in the new order would be equal to Lutherans, was my cue to warn my Lutheran friends that they were likely to lose the shop, but at the time there seemed little to do to stop the momentum. Dr. Hagey and the non-denominational board seemed to have everything going their way.

I have heard that Dr. Hagey used to say that, with his involvement in founding the new university, he had been given a second chance. My real acquaintance with him began when he became president, so I have only hearsay to rely on for information about his first life, but of the new life I know nothing to his discredit—except, of course, that he proceeded with an attempt to appropriate the assets of Waterloo College, and to erase its identity. The manoeuvres and tactics involved in that endeavour were those almost any business man in the community would have used in the takeover of another company. I thought such actions were reprehensible, and I didn't feel he should be allowed to get away with it. That judgement helped to put me on the side of the college in the final struggle from which we emerged, still viable, but with little chance of surviving. "In five years we'll destroy them or absorb them," he is said to have promised his troops. At the end of that time, the survivors and their spouses had a quiet celebration of our continued existence and growing success. He didn't entirely get away with it.

In the early days the struggle for the college was a confusing and complicated battle. Dr. Hagey would sometimes drop into my office for a chat when I was working late on a summer evening. He may have been looking for information, but he talked easily about his plans. At one point he told me he had hired people who had felt badly done by in their previous positions, people who believed their unusual abilities were deliberately ignored or repressed, people, in short who would compete with one another for primacy in the new institution. He didn't add what I did to myself: they were people who would not be troublesome for the administration because they would be kept busy vying with one another for power.

Who had hired them? Officially Dean Schaus of Waterloo College, so far as teaching faculty were concerned. But Dr. Hagey must have had a final veto. There was a rumour that the men hired to set up the new university had, on appointment, given Dr. Hagey their resignations complete except for a date. One expert on co-op education was said to have been hired in spite of a reputation for alcoholism, with the warning that he would be released at the first sign of relapse. I lost touch with the new personnel as I became more involved with the defenders, so I do not know what happened to him, but I am told he does not figure in the history of the University of Waterloo so there may have been some truth in the gossip.

My confusion about who did the hirings comes from the fact that, for a time, Dr. Hagey was president of both institutions, and then when we got our own head, Dr. Hagey seemed to be a *supremo*. Somewhere along the way he had announced what he called "one pot" into which went all assets, and acquisitions thereafter belonged to everyone. That included Seagram Stadium. When it was donated to Waterloo College, Dr. Hagey said he might as well sign for everyone—it would save trouble—with the result one might have expected.

On the day when the move started from our little campus to that of the big university, not only did the newly acquired assets disappear, but so did things that had been acquired by the college earlier. Many of the furnishings, books, etc., had been marked, and so to add to the general ill-feeling of the time there was an added annoyance when college employees arrived with a truck to reclaim typewriters, calculators, etc. that had somehow got onto the wrong campus. It was almost impossible to separate our books from the joint library holdings unless they were theological tomes in German. There are still stories of valuable items of ours which have remained on the University of Waterloo shelves. I have no idea if these tales are true, but I know the fury aroused by the accusations subsided into a bitterness that lasted a long time. Once, on my usual journey to Aberdeen, I took a three-day coach tour for part of it, and found as fellow-travellers a couple of ladies from the University of Waterloo library, whose attitude to me was most cool as soon as they learned I was from WLU. They worked hard to be civilized, and I'm sure no one else noticed anything, but I felt they would have been happier if I had not reminded them of the historical conflict.

Before I go on to discuss more of the new hirings, I should introduce the poor man who became our president from 1959 to 1961. H.M. Axford was a high-principled academic from Winnipeg, of Icelandic origins, who had no idea of what he had gotten into. He did his best in the negotiations with the board of the Associate Faculties and Dr. Hagey, but was far out of his depth. It was rumoured that Axford sat in his office writing poetry when he should have been thinking of ways to get the better of Dr. Hagey. (Certainly I have heard that in the long winters Icelanders used to compose skaldic verses like those of the sagas. Has television ended that custom?) If our president did compose a saga on the harrying of Waterloo College, I should certainly like to see it. When the time came that a few of us banded together to find extraordinary measures to save us from Dr. Hagey, we did not always take the president into our confidence. In his innocence he could have been an embarrassment.

On the surface, negotiations were continuing to define the way a Lutheran arts and science college would become the centre of the new university, while beneath the surface the various denominations were getting into position as adjunct institutions equal in status to the Lutherans. The breaking point came with a letter from Dr. Hagey declaring all the official negotiations null and void. The excuse given was that they had not been ratified by the boards concerned. (I hope a copy of that letter exists. It was crucial to our story.) I recall Dr. Schaus showing the letter to me. He was extremely agitated because he had been negotiating all this time in good faith; I think at that point he had decided that we must go it alone. It may have been around that time that he asked me to stay with the college, promising me what until that time I did not have—a free hand in running the English department. I do not recall when I made the decision to take my chance with the Lutherans. It could not have been too long afterwards.

Meanwhile a lot was going on in within the faculty and even in the student body. Though the story of it will involve some overlapping with what has been said before, I think it will help a reader if I go into some detail in describing these subsidiary, but influential movements.

19

BEFORE TRYING TO SORT OUT THE RUMOURS, plans, and plots on the campus from about 1958 to 1960, let me say that I am aware that any attempt to give structure to the maelstrom of emotions, declarations, and intentions in the winter and spring before our separation from Western and from the University of Waterloo will be false. First, you cannot adequately represent feelings and sorties of the mind except in gesture and cries. Further, to gather as much as possible into only three movements adds to the margin of error and distortion. A historian will try to get some accuracy by using documents. But as I have hinted, I do not think the documents are always close to the original understanding of events by any group. Minutes were sometimes written when memory was not as clear as could be wished, and the various parties, including myself, had their vision distorted by prejudice, self-interest, or (let us concede) principle. Here is one version of the idea of the university as it changed from day to day.

The new look of the college resulted from the new hirings, some made just to augment the faculty for the increased number of students in arts and science, others made to supply courses for the incoming freshman engineers of the Associated Faculties. I am going to leave the Engineering faculty out of this discussion, partly because I didn't know them very well, but mainly because they knew what their function would be as the centre of the new institution: Associated Faculties at first, later the University of Waterloo. Other groups would supply the basic science and mathematics that would be required by their students, and still others would teach the little smattering of arts subjects, such as English. I had no disagreements with the Engineering faculty when I saw them at the meetings of the council that would become the senate, though I didn't hesitate to give my opinions. I wondered if the programme that was being developed would be the best one for students. The new institution would be a pioneer in Canada for its co-operation between engineering school and industry. Students would spend part of the year in manufacturing plants, etc., learning on the job. Their in-school instruction would be narrower than in most colleges of Engineering, with training focused on preparing them for specific types of work. With a brother (from the University of Saskatchewan) and a brother-in-law (from Rensselaer) as graduates in engineering, I knew that education for engineers was usually broad and, though it was directed towards various specialties, the graduates could fit into positions for which they had not been specifically trained. My brother was a mechanical engineer who made his career in oil-refining; my brother-in-law was a chemical engineer who was on the planning side of large-scale construction. I knew too that in the 1950s employers were not pleased with mobility in their work force. I felt that our new faculty was limiting the possibilities for students to please the industrialists and I said so. That may have made me *persona non grata* (a woman and an arts professor pronouncing on engineering). Actually, as I shall explain later, I soon resigned from the council and had little further contact with the planners at the top.

The groups I was really concerned about were three: 1) the scientists, led by a mathematician who got his subject moved into the arts section of the curriculum so that he had a foot in each of the areas that were being developed to support the engineers; 2) a group in the English department hoping to take it over, which I shall call the Lucky Jim party; and 3) the faculty association which openly defied the administration in our last year as a college, and from which was formed a secret group devoted to taking the college from the Lutherans and forcing Dr. Hagey to make them the nucleus of the arts side of what they saw appearing as a new university.

Along with the altercations and scheming, we were trying to prepare our students for the examinations (honours papers still to be marked at Western), and I was not the only faculty member trying to finish a PhD dissertation. The students did very well. That was the year when our English students took the majority of Western's gold medals—they used to give them for each combined course such as English and German, as well as for English alone. I understand that questions were asked in Western's senate about the expense involved in giving away so many gold medals, but since we were leaving them they would not have to worry much more about us. Some of that class of ours went directly to the summer school of the College of Education (luckily for us as it turned out) and others went to good graduate schools, such as Johns Hopkins, and continued to be successful. I now wonder how they and we did it, given all the political turmoil at the time, but we were all young.

The "science party," which included the heads of departments, and the mathematician, regarded itself as the most effective and most influential group. They knew that they would be necessary in the new dispensation, even if only to give basic courses to engineers, but early in the negotiations they had started to hope for more than that. I happen to know this largely because of geography. My office in the then-new teaching building was across the hall from the science laboratories. It was natural for anyone passing by to drop in to pass the time of day and then go on to chat about the latest political developments on campus. Although I knew all of the science faculty, I saw more of one of them than the others—the head of biology (Bruce Kelly) whom I have mentioned earlier as an Irish-Ontarian from near London. I intend to pay a personal tribute to him before I finish my story, but for the moment I'll just mention that we shared one weakness of our common ethnic heritage: a tendency to prefer "yarning" to working. That sometimes goes along with a related tendency to overwork in compensation or perhaps as self-punishment for over indulgence in story telling. Do not misunderstand me. The stories we told were not "stories" such as used to be exchanged at the water cooler and now, I think, figure on the internet. On Kelly's part they often concerned the life of the closely knit community from which he came and which survived probably up until the war. I am afraid the yarns were often rambling digressions. One concerned his father, who seems to have been a pillar of the community, and a large woman, flat-footed and simple-minded, who used to trudge across the field from farm to farm doing odd jobs for her keep. On one of her peregrinations, she attempted to get through a page-wire fence, and being large as well as simple, she got stuck. My friend's father left his team and plow and came to help her—and he too got stuck. A neighbour saw the contretemps and rushed into his house to put through a long ring on the party line, breathlessly begging everyone to get over to the back forty on Kelly's place at once. And they did, converging on the spot of entanglement, helpless with laughter as they watched the ill-matched couple struggling. The story did not include an ending. The orgy of laughter was the point. A whole culture was revealed in the anecdote.

Well, there was a special irony in the fact that the mathematician who had taken the unofficial lead of his party for the new university had come from that same community. His mother had been an "aged" schoolteacher (probably all of forty years old) who had married an even older farmer, and our mathematics head was the result. My friend recalled seeing him, a little boy seated beside his mother in a buggy drawn by a horse. Without any more details, anyone who recalled the old-fashioned Ontario schoolteacher could form the picture: commanding woman, subdued son, reins drawn tightly on family as well as on Dobbin. I should be sorry to confess that the picture often came into my mind when I watched the erstwhile little boy taking charge of the councils of his party. I was not surprised when I heard he was the one who didn't approve of women as department heads.

To be fair I must add that he had become a famous man in the meantime. Before coming to us he had been, I heard, in South America, but somewhere along the way he had acquired the credit for forcing the Ontario school system into the "new math," which may have done something to lessen the respect Ontario youngsters should have had for their elders when it was apparent that a lot of parents would find themselves baffled by their youngsters' homework. He was also a natural leader, not in the sense of asserting himself, but rather by taking charge of a discussion as if a right.

One of the discussions had involved the question of the presidency of the new university. Someone dropped into my office to inform me that they (the science group, I gathered) had decided not to "dump Hagey." (I am not sure of the words, but that was the meaning.) They had decided they could "handle him." I listened with interest as always, but kept my thoughts to myself. I rather thought Dr. Hagey was in charge of whatever dumping was to be done.

Another decision that I heard over my desk was that because the college campus was so small, there would have to be another site for the new institution. It was the head groundsman who was my informant at that time. It did not occur to me that such a move would involve real estate transactions that would have an effect on the economic life of the community, as well as adding a lot to the landscape amenities of Waterloo.

Was it this group to whom Dr. Hagey gave the news that they wouldn't have to be bothered by the Waterloo College board much longer? Perhaps it included the Engineering faculty at that point. I wonder if minutes were kept, and if so how Hagey's reassurance appeared in them. This now seems vague, I realize, but all we had were speculations and rumour.

As rumours grew and uncertainty built, someone—it may have been I—suggested to the science group that we should get together and talk frankly. This was a private meeting, away from boards and administrations, and without attempt to make political advantage. I cannot say that it was exactly friendly. The scientists new to the campus made it clear that they detested and distrusted any church connection with their discipline. I was surprised by the emotion involved in some of the declarations. Did it come from previous experience? As I have said before, I had seen little of any attempt to muzzle science on our campus. My course on nineteenth-century literature, which included arguments in favour of Darwin by Huxley, always passed off without a ripple of disapproval. I *had* heard of one clergyman who must have taken American Literature as a student because he supposedly stated that the professor who lectured on it should have given a Christian turn to Bryant's "Thanatopsis," but I was told that as a joke. The important fact was that this influential group insisted that religion should be shut away in church colleges and not allowed to come within arm's length of science. I recall exclaiming at that point, "You are asking us to cut our own throats." "No," replied the head of chemistry immediately, "but I'll lend you the knife." There was no hope of a compromise. The Lutheran Church would have to give up all hope of being the centre of the new university if that university was to have a science faculty.

20

THE LUCKY JIM PARTY DESERVES A SECTION TO ITSELF, not only because of its importance in the movement toward two universities, but because it helps to explain the atmosphere of the late 1950s in universities here as well as in the UK where the book *Lucky Jim* found its characters and plot. I have already described the Crowe case. The Lucky Jim episode was our version of it. I thank heaven that more pressing troubles caused the episode to end not with a bang but a non-fire. The professor in a distant university who had trained one of our Jims—not wisely and not at all well—told me ominously at a later meeting of the Learneds, "We'll have to get on that campus"—"we" being the CAUT, and the reason being to ferret out a complaint since one had not been officially filed, but the principals had lost interest by that time and were, as they say now, getting on with their lives. The CAUT later did come to our campus but the visit ended amiably.

Before I remind you of the original *Lucky Jim*, a book published in 1953 by Kingsley Amis and later made into a film, let me explain

the joke. In our tiny English department by 1958 we had three Jims.
(We have had two more since then.) For a time it seemed that we
were hiring only Jims and Margarets. I began to wonder if the anti-
discrimination police might come after me for an explanation. But
to return to the original *Lucky Jim*, it is a sort of fairy tale, if I may
use that term for a story about a young man whose interests seem
to be booze and girls, who finds himself in a stuffy English Department in a strait-laced university and pursued by an acidic and strag-
gly woman. He is rescued by an avuncular rich man and departs to
promises of affluence with a fetching blonde on his arm—or is it in
his arms? (The video, if it is still in circulation, can be seen as a
worms-eye view of university life in the 1950s. Apparently Philip
Larkin sent Amis many of the details used in the book.)

I saw the film before I glanced at the book so its images are those
that have stayed with me. I was much amused by it all, but with
some reservations. It was all very well to see life in a university
from the viewpoint of the lowliest lecturer, convinced of his supe-
riority to all around him, but caught out at every turn. Mine was
the point of view of the head, with a job to do and with recruits who
were not going to become part of the team. The moral of the
book/film was that the whole academic enterprise should be
scrapped. Mine was that, in the meantime, there were students with
three or four years to spend under our eyes, for which they would
thank or damn us later.

One of our three Jims was my assistant who had been chosen by
Professor Woodhouse in the beginning and who was, until his death,
the centre of gravity of the English department. Through all the
events that led to the split and thereafter, his attitude and actions
were exemplary.

The two other Jims were the lucky ones. They had come from
the University of British Columbia, and so far as I know were born
in the province which I have come to regard as a distinct society.
Once I was caught in a record snowfall there, and realized something of the way the dangers of mountains and sea have worked on
a whole people to produce a society which is more egalitarian and
less formalized than that in the rest of Canada, especially in Southern Ontario where our Jims found themselves. Both were, I believe,

sprung from the militant British working class that had figured in disputes in the BC maritime unions. The first Jim was more obviously of that background. In our early acquaintance he told me with some satisfaction that he had enjoyed his stint in the peace-time air force because he and his friend had amused themselves by thinking up ways to use the regulations to annoy the officers. (Barrack room lawyers, I think the species is called.) He carried his air force manner over to our campus. He stood erect, at ease, and seemed at the same time respectful yet immovable. (I have seen the same type at least twice, once on a station platform in Toronto when the light-eyed agents of the railway union refused to let us through, though their strike was not due to start for another hour, by which time we would have been safe from their constraint. My other experience with the kind was an opportunity to observe a high union official from BC on shipboard. He had that same plain certainty, that straight-eyed air of not being moved that must have infuriated negotiators when he met them in disputes involving his union.)

Jim number 1 did the jobs assigned to him adequately, and was never in active opposition to me or to the administration. He just carried on by constitutional means to become head of our faculty association, and his aims and achievements there I shall describe when I come to discuss the part that body played in events leading up to the split. When we separated from the University of Waterloo, he was one of the first, if not the first person to be hired for the University of Waterloo English department. He had caught the attention of the (Australian) head of Engineering whose prescription for the English to be taught to his students was that the texts must be paperbacks. (Do you recall those glossy covered little books that tried to sum up new ventures in ideas?) I know nothing of his career on the other campus. I rather suspect that the organization there did not give as much room for faculty politics as was available at little Waterloo College. Dr. Hagey was not unobservant and was not likely to leave space for grassroots activists. I think we can say though that our man was Lucky Jim number 1.

Jim number 2 was more like Amis's original but better. I hope I shall be forgiven for giving some details of his career—my only excuse is that it makes what strikes me as a good story—1950s style.

I felt no ill-will to him, and it may be that he regarded me with a sort of exasperated affection—exasperated because I was so unlike his idea of a head—someone to get drunk with, and suffer a hangover with, coming out of both experiences as brothers.

First, I could never be a brother, second I have been drunk only twice; in fact I now realize that what I thought were the effects of too much wine at dinner in a hotel in Riva were probably advance warnings of the food poisoning that hit me before the night was over. The first occasion was at a party given by one of our students. On arrival at his apartment the bottle one had brought in response to the BYOB invitation was snatched away, and the contents poured into a large container to join the wine, vodka, whiskey, gin, etc. already mixed up there. Even with my minuscule imbibing of the punch I became somewhat fuzzy, but I don't recall whooping and hollering as the neighbours said guests did at parties given in the home of Jim number 1. In fact, I drove home at a late hour (with shame I recall it) but very carefully.

Because my acquaintance with Jim number 2 developed when I forgot I was responsible for the department, he afforded me considerable amusement. His family had originated in the Shetlands and, though I had no personal knowledge of the islands and their inhabitants, I had seen his physical and emotional type before from areas not as far north. He would have been a perfect choice for the main character in the film *Lucky Jim*: perhaps a little under medium height, physical articulation a bit slack (unlike the military compactness of Jim number 1), darkish hair that wanted to wave, good (meaning well-cut) features that I recall as never still, all surrounded by a navy blue suit that may have been slept in. I remember him as always gesturing but that may be because he was rarely without a cigarette in hand and was always flicking ash.

Now as I think about him at some distance I find myself visualizing his ancestors standing—or leaping up and down—on a cliff, shouting maledictions and throwing a few rocks at my ancestors as they went about their business of beaching a shallow-drawing boat in a creek before moving inland for a spot of pillage. Then I just accepted his singularity as something given—not to be analyzed in the way it would be now, probably by searching in childhood history, whether psychological or circumstantial.

Very early the rumour went around the campus that he had never got over losing the girl he loved to another man, but he was not exactly lonely at Waterloo College. Students and colleagues were fond of him. An alumnus recently told me, "I had quite an affection for him, he was so different." Different, that is, from our sturdy, steady students who were moving on the usual tracks to worthy careers. One of his colleagues used to tease him by calling him a missionary (one of the most objectionable words in Jim's vocabulary) and indeed he seemed to have a fanatical belief in his calling to preach against two things: chastity and religion. Whenever he saw a dawning relationship, as we might call it now, he felt he must persuade the couple into bed, not realizing that they were quite capable of thinking of that themselves. His other object of attack was the Christian religion in any form (Canada had not yet become officially multicultural). His lectures in English were an opportunity to rail against Milton's God, rather, I thought, in the manner of Empson, though the book of that name did not appear until 1961. Jim called himself a humanist, and wrote a summary of his faith for the *College Cord*, but to my dismay he demonstrated a not very deep understanding of that belief or of any other.

You may wonder how the Lutheran campus received his message. Generally it was with amusement. I never heard a complaint. One student said he enjoyed the lectures, "They were such a challenge to my faith," he told me. There may have been complaints to Dean Schaus, but he too seemed amused, and protective of someone so obviously at sea. Perhaps his general ineffectuality was the secret of Jim's popularity. For instance, when he finally got up enough money and courage to buy and drive a car, a wheel fell off on one of his first ventures.

Though he had found himself early to be unlucky in love, as I said he was not lonely at our college. He shared an apartment with one of our male students, an ex-Mountie, and he paid for an apartment for another, this time a young woman. One of his less sophisticated colleagues remarked on both facts to me, citing them as examples of Jim's benevolence. I wasn't so sure. It was an odd experience to give a seminar to a group that included the ex-Mountie, who steadily regarded me with a challenge in his eyes, and the girl, a sweet little thing who seemed totally confused.

When Jim number 2 left us, he sent the girl to his friends at his old university with the injunction to take care of her, as they told me. Now and then they gave me news of "Jim's girl," as they called her, and finally reported that she was satisfactorily married. Privately I felt that, of all the people in his story, she had probably suffered most, but in those days we didn't feel that the private lives of lecturers were our responsibility unless they were inordinately scandalous. My own opinion was that Jim's missionary zeal for sex may have come from his belief that, as the folk-singers of the era had it, he had "lost [his] true love/For courtin' too slow." On the side of religion I suspected early indoctrination with one of the more unkind varieties of Presbyterianism. Neither was any of my business.

Jim number 2 unfortunately became the centre of what almost became our own version of the Crowe case, but I shall leave that for a minute to tell you of the happy ending of his story, as far as I know it—which is enough for a romantic comedy or film.

When this Jim left us he went to Saskatchewan. The head there was a good friend of mine, so though I wanted Jim to have a job, I didn't want to hand on our problem to the U of S. My recommendation was as honest as I could make it. I don't recall the wording now, but it may have been like this. "The candidate can do good work under careful supervision." Carlyle King was no patsy even if he was noted for his left-wing politics, as I noted earlier, and he would keep an eye on a young lecturer. As it turned out he didn't need to. The university had mandatory yearly testing for TB for everyone on campus. Jim was found to be infected and was whisked away to the sanatorium just outside the city. No, this is not the story of *The Magic Mountain*. By this time remedies had been found which worked for everyone who wasn't allergic to them. The sanatorium was a pleasant place, and within easy reach of the friends Jim had already made in his new post. I heard that he had all the visitors he needed to make time pass happily. What more could he want?

I have never heard the details, but soon all his acquaintances knew that a miracle had happened. The lost sweetheart turned up, now without the husband but with four children. The final picture is of Jim as husband and father (I am pretty sure they got married) setting off with his family, probably towards the sunset. If I wanted to end on a comic note I would invent a departure in a car, only to have the wheel fall off, with the last shot showing the whole family regarding the fallen axle in disbelief. But we must stick to facts. My informants never offered any details after the *peripeteia*. (We used to show off by using that term for a sudden and unexpected dramatic turning point.)

But now to the problems. Jim number 2 had indeed been hired to teach engineers, but his speciality was said to be Old English, and though I had dealt successfully with Western's prescriptions for honours students in that subject, I was not a specialist, so I gladly ceded the course to him. Our students at that time were to be famous as our winners of gold medals—one had been the top student in the grade 13 examinations for the whole province, and they could estimate an instructor's grasp of a subject in very little time. Also they had friends and relations at Western and had access to old examination papers. After some quiet research they sent a deputation to me to report that they would have no chance of passing the examination if Jim number 2 was their only source of information about Old English. My duty was to remove him at once and take over the course myself. Politics dictated that for many reasons I should not publicly disgrace him or the university that had guaranteed his competence. I prefer openness, but have learned that the battles of life, and especially of the academy, require diplomacy. I broke one of my own rules about never interfering in a colleague's course, and undercover delivered to the students all the resource material I could assemble—and left it to them to arrange secret seminars where they would teach each other. It worked, but though I told no one, I am sure the English department at Western heard of the whole affair through the student connections I have mentioned.

My other problem with Jim was his refusal to teach composition. The first-year English course at that time required that a large percentage of time was to be spent on writing. He never actually refused, he just didn't teach it, and when I inquired he would evade the question. Again, I hadn't informed Western, but academic gossip does get around. At one of our twice-yearly conferences with Western, the man in charge of first-year English asked Jim directly, "What did you do about the composition?" receiving the reply, "I treated it with the contempt which it deserved," a sentence which almost immediately spread over both campuses—and of which I am sure Jim was very proud.

That is, until the senate at Western accepted a motion that his contract should not be renewed. Now we really had a dilemma. How far did Western's authority go and how much was the prerogative of the federated college? Our dean who was sensitive about matters of jurisdiction wanted to refuse to obey Western. I may have indicated earlier that he had, too, a pastoral concern for black sheep and a respect for rebels.

Our president was on the other side. I didn't mention that when I recall Jim standing up a little shakily to speak at a meeting it was usually to bait authority (mostly the president) with remarks bordering on insolence, and certainly expressing impertinence, as he looked around triumphantly at the friends who would protect him from his proper punishment. I don't know how the president kept his temper, but he did. I wonder if he thought of *his* ancestors, who were as likely to have made landfall in the Shetlands as were mine, and what *they* would have done if a cheeky native had been so impudent. That is fantasy. In reality he now grabbed the opportunity and declared for dismissal.

And me? I felt I must get more information. I was prepared to keep Jim, but to assign him to courses for engineers, avoiding both Old English and composition. I had not yet learned that a soft answer does not always turn away wrath, and that compromise sometimes makes a situation worse. Anyway I needed to get more information and some advice. I called the friendly Dean of Arts at Western and asked if I could come to London to see him. No, I couldn't be seen on campus. I would have to go to his home to meet him. Astonished, I agreed, and was more dismayed to see that he was really frightened. "What do they want? Blood?" he asked. He was a little afraid for me, but more for himself. I have never completely understood this, though the revelations about Western's opposition to the intentions of the Ontario government to found a competing university in Waterloo may be in the picture. Any suggestion that Western had stretched its authority over a federated college might have been an argument for reducing his power—but I really don't think that was his concern. He was terrified of the CAUT. In discussing the plight of United College in Winnipeg, I hope I have conveyed the possibilities for harm to a university if the new faculty body could put a place under an interdict. Before long we learned that the resolution of the senate regarding non-renewal of Jim's contract had disappeared from the minutes. So where did that leave us?

The CAUT had not yet come into the affair. I believe that, as happened with the Crowe case, someone of some standing, preferably on another campus, would have had to file an official complaint first. Our faculty association had other things on its collective mind, but the news that the president had "fired poor Jim" brought out the mass feeling that something must be done. I had not fought against the dismissal—so I must be to blame. I never heard directly anything from our faculty association, but rumour told me that they had sent deputations to campuses around us, but not with any clear objectives. Should a complaint be filed charging me? our president—who was just obeying orders? or Western?—when the relevant documentary evidence had disappeared? I did hear that when they addressed the faculty association at Guelph, a red-headed friend of mine (as much an iconoclast as they) gave them a witty tongue-lashing, I think because their complaints were not thought through or rationally presented.

The danger was certainly there. What happened to United College could have happened to us, but events on campus had reached a state of *sauve qui peut* where Dr. Hagey was picking up a few survivors of what seemed to be the shipwreck of Waterloo College, and the rest had to look after themselves. The campaign against the college on Jim's behalf fizzled out, but his story came to a happy ending.

21

The expected shipwreck of Waterloo College didn't happen, but change came about at the end of the third branch of our story which I called that of the faculty association and its attempt to wrest control of the college from the Lutheran Synod.

I returned to the college late in the summer of 1959 for what was to be its last year to find that it had changed. So had I. I had made an unforeseen flight in June to the deathbed of one parent, and about six weeks later repeated the flight for the other parent, though arriving too late. It was not a cheerful time, but one bright spot had been the sympathy of my colleagues which they had expressed on both occasions with a profusion of flowers. My relatives, when they mentioned my having to go back to live among strangers, remarked that the flowers had shown that at least I had friends in Ontario.

But in the new atmosphere on campus I was not sure of my place. The faculty association seemed to be the centre of decision-making with a new drive and new goals. Jim number 1 had become the president, and he was surrounded by a purposeful group that included not only Jim number 2 but the head of the history department and his friends. It appeared that they had been pulled together to fight the recent election in which the historian had run as a candidate. The campaign had gained our faculty association group some support in the community among Trades and Labour Council members, and left-wing sympathizers in general. On campus we now seemed to have divided into two parties, one made up of the historian and followers (including a few Lutherans) and the more influential Lutherans such as Dr. Overgaard, the Littles, and the chaplain, Dr. Dolbeer, among others, and myself.

My isolation may have come from the Lucky Jim Party to some extent, but the students had earlier detected a more serious division. In their traditional year-end joke version of the *College Cord*, they had printed a clever parody of something like a medieval battle, including an attack on a castle, one side mine and the other led by the historian. I was much amused because the spoof was very well done, but I was also a little puzzled because there was no reason given for our opposition. I just assumed that in our lectures we had somehow taken opposite views of some historical movement or event. I later learned from an alumnus that the students had detected a political difference. As I have often said, we had some unusually sharp students then, who had apparently assessed their professors' political views and had rated the historian as left of centre and myself as to the right. This was the more unexpected because I had studiously avoided advocating *any* political stance in my background lectures for English texts. The historian it seems had let his preferences show. Some time after that an English and history honours student came to my office in order to share his disquiet about a seminar he had attended in the historian's house. There the host had disclosed to a select group of students his conviction that reform could never be brought about by democratic means, but only by genuine revolution like the Russian one. Remember how afraid we were then of appearing as imitators of Senator McCarthy. I reassured the student, I'm not sure how, and remained not very concerned. I didn't think there were too many possible recruits to the Communist Party among our students, and besides wasn't the CP legal in Canada?

One thing I know: I had never advocated the Russian Soviet system, for reasons which I have given already, and the historian had made no secret of his fascination with communist Russia. He reported on his happy visit there as an Intourist guest, and was seriously studying the language. That may have helped the students to make their political diagnoses.

My first awareness that my position had changed on campus came at the first faculty association meeting of the new academic year. I had been a charter member and had valued my connection with the new symbol of academic solidarity. Under the chairmanship of Jim number 1, the meeting got underway with a financial report. When discussion was called, someone immediately rose and denounced the amount spent on flowers. Not only had I been a drain on the treasury, but someone else had lost his father and had thus been the occasion of raising expenditures. There was no further comment, but I sat in shock, and as soon as possible I left and made out a cheque for the amount spent on me which I consigned to Jim. I didn't go back to a meeting of our faculty association until we became independent, but I did get my cheque back. At the next meeting my Lutheran friends, now not inhibited by my presence, had started a lovely dispute. Jim wanted to keep the cheque, but the meeting decided that it should be returned. For a long time I could hardly bear to think about the occasion, and ever after I avoided if possible my encounter with Jim number 1 whom I regarded as the initiator of the whole thing. Now viewing it after forty or more years, I realize that the incident was part of a campaign that would lead to a showdown between the two campus parties, and that if the new president of the association could put one member of the other party off the field, the dirty tactics would be worth it. He had a long-term campaign in mind and could miss no opportunity to weaken the opposition. I should have stayed in there to fight. Had he guessed that I would get out of *that* struggle at least? I had never seen political warfare carried out at that level and could not get adjusted to it, which was too bad because there was going to be more of the same.

Socially I seemed to get on as well as before with the historian's party, though once I was hurt when a professor of French said to me, "Why don't you get away and see something?" He and his French wife and the historian (among others) left for Europe each summer, returning often just as the term was opening, while I had for several years been responsible for my ailing parents—and for my dissertation which I was still patching up. But I hadn't thought my classes had suffered from what might have been considered my insularity—and I *had* "seen Paree."

Before I begin to describe the final struggle, I want to mention that I was in no psychological or perhaps even physical condition for the war ahead. In time I would recover—but time I did not have. I had removed myself from the faculty association, and before long would officially retire from the senate. The second retreat was the more ignominious. I should have stayed as a voice for those who insisted that the original plan of structuring the new university around the Lutheran college would be maintained, but, as I have shown earlier, that plan grew more and more untenable.

The meetings of the small body that was the precursor of the University of Waterloo senate were unlike anything I had ever participated in before. I wondered why I felt so upset shortly after each meeting began, and then realized that a number of the members were deliberately trying to make others lose their tempers so that they would be at a disadvantage in the negotiations that were going on. The inflammatory remarks were usually made in a joking tone, but the intention to wound was unmistakable. I wonder how many antacid pills were required to settle stomachs after some of our gatherings. I couldn't take it. I felt I should save myself for another day and so I resigned.

I was concerned for the fate of one of the members, Bruce Kelly, the head of our biology area. The scientists' party was so obviously in favour of taking the college from the Lutherans that its members didn't have to join either campus party, but Kelly still felt a tie to his colleagues at Waterloo College, while wanting to be fair to the new institution. He was not insulated against the malice that, to me at least, seemed to govern the meetings leading up to the split. He called me once by telephone to say that Dean Schaus was no longer a friend—this was during the negotiations regarding the relationship between the college and the new university which Dr. Hagey later annulled. The dean could hold his own in acrimonious discussions, though the cost was apparent in his subsequent early physical deterioration. For Kelly the price was paid first in a heart attack, I think during a meeting after his senate group had separated from us, and then by his death which I am convinced was hastened by the atmosphere in which he had to work. He had called me not long before his final collapse, not with any definite information but conveying an impression of unease that worried me—as it turned out rightly. I was not impressed by the funeral his new colleagues gave him.

For a time there was still some attempt to show that the Lutheran college, including its faculty and administration, would be the centre of the new university. The Associate Faculties now had their own board, as of December 2, 1959 while the Lutheran Board remained in charge of the college, but boundaries were becoming indistinct, and as I said earlier, financial resources now were, as Dr. Hagey put it, "in one pot." The arrangement looked to be sensible enough, yet some of us became more and more uneasy.

We were all called to a joint faculty meeting held in one of the fresh buildings on the new campus. (The date must be in minutes somewhere.) I drove down in my little vw Beetle and parked, but could not bring myself to get out of the car. I cannot describe the desolation I felt. Now I think I can trace it to a conviction that, from now on, university life as I had known it was coming to an end. Universities had for me stood for order, fairness, even for ceremony. My *alma mater* was a raw prairie place, it is true, but the original president and a number of faculty members from its early days were still there, and the tone they had brought to it from much older traditions still held. The president's wife entertained all the female students at lunch (I think in their graduating year) in small groups where many of us for the first time were served formally by the elderly maid in white cap and apron. I am sure it was done so that we would experience a life such as we had only read about in our eighteenth- and nineteenth-century texts. In our four-hour seminars in English, a similar, but younger maid would bring in the tea tray at halftime and the professor would ask one of his female students to pour. In turn we all practiced being hostesses, making sure everyone had the right mixture of milk and sugar and tea, and seeing that everyone had biscuits or whatever the treat was. No wonder I regarded a university as a place of ease plus formality, to be emulated in my own life.

My time in the Diocesan School in Regina combined discipline and relaxed formality with "the beauty of holiness" (a term I am sure has now vanished from our hymn books). Morning and evening the girls assembled in their grey and blue uniforms and chapel veils for matins and vespers. I recall that a Jewish father brought his daughter to be registered at the school. When the Sister Superior reminded him that the girl could not be excused from chapel attendance, his reply was that she would be a better Jew for it, and he was right. In the future when, as a wife and mother, she would light the Sabbath candles she would also be recalling something of the ceremonial gestures that had become a habit at school.

Waterloo College was a cruder place, of course, but each morning one might attend the chapel service where, for a short time, everyday concerns and manners were traded for decorum and "decency," meaning as Webster's reminds us, "conformity to standards of taste, propriety, or quality." This tradition appealed to me, especially since at the Diocesan School and at Waterloo College, things were done under Milton's "Great Taskmaster's eye." We didn't stop at all times to ask ourselves what the Almighty might think of what we were doing, but there was a sense of having to answer to a higher authority than the board of governors.

As I sat in my little car I think I was sensing that all of that tradition was ending, and that the new university would have different aims—as indeed would the new age. Waterloo Lutheran University when it came, was not Waterloo College writ large. I think we still had a sense of responsibility to something transcendent, but we thought more than before about competition, practical advantages, and marketing our product instead of upholding standards of taste and propriety. I wonder now how long we kept up the customs of having teas for the female students where they learned to be "ladies" in a setting that prepared them for their roles in women's clubs and church celebrations. And where is the university tea service?

As I look at what I have just written I know that today in 2004 very few born after 1950 will have any idea of what I have been describing. The canon of English Literature, which as we used to joke went from Beowulf to Virginia Woolf, was the basis for our education, though by my time we had a course in American Literature as well. (Canadian Literature in Saskatchewan had made it into the high school curriculum, but only in small examples.) My romantic notions of "English" were symptoms of infection perhaps from the "Metaphysicals," as well as from Shakespeare among others, who could reconcile the spiritual and the material in their art, which seemed to young and idealistic students a good enough prescription for life itself.

I had had further exposure to the virus in my two years as a teacher at the convent school and four years living in the purlieus of the mother house where the nuns walking in meditation in the garden would cross our paths as we dashed off to our graduate classes at the University of Toronto. I knew that the nun with her whole mind fixed on the sacred would, in a few minutes, be attending with

equal attention to the laundry or the kitchen, and I knew too that
the vow of obedience was not always easy to keep. (Poverty and
chastity may not have been as troublesome. I wonder what Darwin
would have considered the first sin). But I felt the underlying determination to keep the holy always in view. In the world we were
entering there would be more of the profane than the sacred.

I did at last get myself into the joint meeting and was not reassured. The anti-Lutheran group were there in a mood which nowadays might be called triumphalist (a word which seems to have
been resurrected for occasions like these). They were ostentatiously
rude to authority, their demeanour demonstrating the conviction
that they were going to be the commanding centre of the new university, and that no one should stand in their way. (Now I realize
that they may have had some inspiration in a glass or two before
the meeting. Then I just sat horrified.) I left with Dr. Overgaard, and
when we would not be overheard I said, "Herman, this will never
work." "Yes, I know," he said glumly, "but what can we do?" It
looked hopeless, but he and others were doing a great deal behind
the scenes; that story shall be postponed in order to reveal the end
of the story for our anti-Lutheran party.

They must have been working hard and secretly because it
became more and more clear that the new arrangements had no
place for a Lutheran university college in the University of Waterloo. I think it was at the end of the academic year when the head of
the Department of Romance Languages came to my office, looking
a bit upset. "Here is something you ought to see," he said as he put
a paper on my desk. It was a petition, or perhaps more a declaration, that if the Lutherans did not give up Waterloo College by a
certain date, which was stated, the undersigned would resign. The
names included practically every faculty member except myself and
the activist Lutherans.

I could hardly believe our luck. With the rebel party, as I had
seen them perform at the joint meeting, it would be almost impossible to develop a successful academic agglomeration; without them
we might have a chance as an independent institution.

And here I should stop to explain what, in my view, was the difference between a church college such as those planned for the new

university, and a church-related university. In the college, students of one faith would live together, I am sure with mutual benefit and support. In the university, as it had been in Waterloo College, students would be drawn from all faiths and races available, and in the residences they would all have to learn how to live with others of different creeds or none at all. It was more likely too that, in a university such as we envisioned, you could avoid drawing students from one class in society only. For example, one of the Honours English graduates in my first year at Waterloo College was the son of the chauffeur of one of the city's leading industrialists. His fellow students came from quite different levels of society with no strain involved in their common interest in England. I would never have been happy in a strictly denominational institution, but a larger version of the old Waterloo College could prove interesting—and worthwhile.

It was obvious that some of the movers of the petition had argued that I should be given a chance to join the rebel group, and for their intervention I was grateful, but it was not for me. It must have been when I returned the paper to Jim number 1 that I said, "Do you realize that you have given your resignations?" "Oh, no, we have not," he replied shortly, because he was sure the board would never contemplate losing him and his friends—but he was wrong. They *had* resigned. The split was in effect and they had no refuge. I would have let matters stand there (to my shame, I admit it) but Dean Schaus who was a true pastor wrote to each offering a position in the new Lutheran institution in the new term—an invitation which several took up—at least two going on with us to retirement, though not, I think happily. One was much more left-wing and said at least once that he felt he had had to keep his convictions to himself. The other never seemed easy with us, but his interest had been, I believe in retaining a job, not in ideology. And the rest?

Their ultimatum had no effect, of course, and gossip had it that the historian then went "down the hill" (as we came to describe visits to the new campus) and threatened Dr. Hagey with exposure of the "land deal," if he did not hire as a body the signatories to the petition. Gossip said that Dr. Hagey laughed at him.

The so-called land deal has not entered into my story because I have little first-hand knowledge of it, though I knew someone who had researched it carefully at the land office, and who was convinced that there was some conflict of interest in the acquisition of the new campus. (See Ken McLaughlin, *Waterloo: The Unconventional Founding of an Unconventional University.*) I was once overheard by a supporter of the new university when I was speaking somewhat carelessly about the matter, and was threatened with a suit for slander, so even at this late date I should prefer to have the facts in my hand before drawing any conclusions.

I had stopped reading the *K-W Record* at the time when I was told that it had published an article on the land deal on the basis of information submitted by the Trades and Labour Council, so the historian's friend may have made his threat good. But I heard later that "they" had been forced to withdrawn the accusation. Did "they" refer to the newspaper or to the Trades and Labour people? I can only add that the community in general was not likely to be hard on anyone who was just making a buck. When one of the three young men in English heard the story, he went out and bought shares in the company handling the land transfer. He was the sensible one who didn't get involved in controversy. I am sure he went on to succeed in whatever activity followed his time at Waterloo College.

I believe that the first sign that Dr. Hagey would hire some of our faculty came when a professor of German went "down the hill." He hadn't been too easy in his connection with the plotters. As a refugee from Siberia after the war, he may have had a sense of déjà vu in regard to the political activities on campus, and I can see why he wanted to have things settled.

That first break led to a steady pilgrimage down the hill as a great many of the plotters went individually to ask for positions. Some were hired. (I have mentioned Lucky Jim number 1.) Others not. When the historian's father died I wrote the usual letter to him— but with some feeling of sympathy too. He replied thanking me, but adding sadly, "If only we had stuck together we would have succeeded." He had either forgotten—or had never known—that I had not originally been included in the rebel group, and that when given a chance I had not joined. I had the impression that he had been

working in a sort of dream, inspired by books, without much awareness of life in the arena. We heard he had accepted a job in a women's
college in the USA, and in time he came back to a position in Montreal. As I may have mentioned before, I was told he took a teaching post in the Jesuit college.

Some who were not accepted by the University of Waterloo were
unhappy because they had not gone with their friends. One actually wept. Among the other things I was learning from the whole
experience was the intensity of feeling that can exist in a "buddy"
situation. There were strong bonds of loyalty and affection in this
predominately all-male world.

I haven't too much information about what was happening down
the hill but I had been informed quite early that the men who at
that time seemed to be running the new university were quite early
making plans about hiring or not hiring Waterloo College faculty.

I cannot place the time when one of our graduates who was an
assistant to the registrar of the new university stopped his car beside
me as I was walking on King Street and urgently asked me to step
in. He then drove slowly in residential streets where we would not
be recognized, and told me his boss had handed him a list of Waterloo College faculty, saying, "Here are some people who won't be
around very long," meaning once the two institutions were merged.
My name was prominent on the list.

Some years later I was at a party where I met again a woman
who, at the time I describe, had been the registrar's secretary. I asked
her if she could now find it ethical to break confidentiality and tell
me if there really had been such a list. Looking very uncomfortable
she said that I had indeed been on it.

My feeling of annoyance when I was first told came partly from
the fact that I could tell no one at that time that I would not be on
the new faculty even if invited. Further, I had just survived a year
of having the registrar as a student in an English Honours seminar
which he was taking to upgrade his standing as a General Arts Major
at the University of Toronto. I'm sure he didn't know I had given
two of the basic general English courses for his university, and I realized that he had expected an Honours seminar at an inferior institution to be a walkover. He really didn't have the time or the interest

needed to do well in an advanced seminar, but I'm sure he attributed
his not very high standing to my incompetence. He went on later
to a successful career as a civil servant, probably still thinking that
he had paid me back for not giving him an A.

Had he shown my friend the list hoping that I would hear of it?
Certainly rumour was busily running between the two campuses.
I was told that at one meeting regarding faculty, when my name
came up Dr. Hagey said he had no objection to me. The mathematician, the *éminence grise*, made the remark to which I have alluded
before, that no woman should be head of a department. As an
appointed head, my status was part of my contract and they seemingly felt they would have to honour it if they hired me.

When our connection with Western ended, there was a sort of
state dinner in London for the administration and faculty of the college and of the associate body. The Highlander who had promised to
give me a refuge (actually Islander which is even more fey) shook
himself out of a daze and said to me, sitting beside him, something
like, "I can see the future, and all will be well for you." You never
know whether they are having you on—or really divining, but I do
not entirely ignore the soothsayer—and this time he was right
though no reasonable person could have guessed it at that time.

This has been a lot about me and about a non-event but I'll add
one more anecdote or perhaps two, to add confession to my relations with the University of Waterloo. A friend who has recently
retired from WLU has a brother who was in the beginning a junior
mathematician in the Associate Faculties and later had a career at
the U of W. When I met him several years ago he reminded me that
we had been colleagues and he was most cordial. My friend later
remarked that he had a high regard for me. I recalled my defiance of
authority at the proto-senate meetings I have mentioned and wondered if news of my championship of students and of the rank and
file in general had been common knowledge among young lecturers
who had very little opportunity to protest themselves.

A number of years later I received a mysterious call from someone describing himself as being on the University of Waterloo Engineering faculty. He had heard of my intention to introduce a study
of the technical side into our courses on Communication, and he

offered me any help he could give. We had just hired a man with European and Canadian experience in that area, so I declined but felt grateful that someone "down the hill" or "at the other place," as we sometimes came to call it, was not an enemy. Because relations between the two institutions didn't immediately get better when we separated. And that is another story.

22

WHAT WAS THE LOYALIST PARTY DOING in the meantime? That story properly belongs to the Lutherans. I was not involved in most of what went on but I was kept informed of a great deal. Dr. Overgaard, who can be called the leader of the Lutheran party, usually asked for advice and tested different approaches before deciding on a course of action, and I was one of his "ears."

In 1996 I was in touch with Dr. Overgaard who was one of the two or three people remaining who could remember some of the details of events of 1959-60. He reminded me of several threads in the narrative which may not be apparent to a researcher depending only on official records. His campaign had the goal of preventing Waterloo College from being reduced to a little residential institution for Lutherans, which would probably teach support courses for the seminary and religious knowledge for arts students. There were other campaigns related to the primary one. As I mention them I may not follow the best order, but at the time there was *no* order. Everything was happening at once.

Before proceeding to some description of events I should perhaps explain what was at stake for Dr. Overgaard and the loyalist Lutherans. They were fighting for the continuation of an institution in which they had invested not only their intellectual labour but also their aspiration for the future. They hoped to build an educational foundation that would put the Canadian Lutheran church on a level with the American Lutherans whose pride was in their colleges and universities. Waterloo College was an asset—not only in financial terms—that the Canadian Lutheran Church could not afford to lose.

As an outsider I felt that the Lutherans deserved to have the chance to make *their* contribution to Canadian higher education, as the Presbyterians had done through founding Queen's, the Baptists with McMaster, or the Church of England in Canada through Western (Huron College), and through the University of Toronto (King's College). Lutherans had been victimized at the time of the Clergy Reserves when some of their churches in the Eastern Townships were taken from them and given to what is now the Anglican Communion. Locally, as I pointed out earlier, Lutheranism had been equated with the German enemy. Dr. Overgaard's ancestors had thought of the Lutheran Church as the state church, an integral part of being Norwegian, and that approach was shared by a great many Canadians from Northern Europe who were now in Canada, surrounded by fellow citizens who had no concept of the contributions to Western civilization of Lutheran music, literature, art, and philosophy, as well as theology. I was cheering on the sidelines for a possible Canadian institution that could share in that heritage and pass it on to students of all kinds and beliefs. (By the 1960s the institution that succeeded Waterloo College—Waterloo Lutheran University—was the largest Lutheran college in North America.)

A new aspect of the struggles for and against the incorporation of the Lutheran entity into the new University of Waterloo came from the AUCC (the Association of Universities and Colleges of Canada). Dr. Gibson, at that time president of Queen's and of the association, came to Waterloo on December 2, 1959, to speak to the Lutheran board in order to persuade them to stop Dr. Hagey's plan to found a new university in Ontario. From the viewpoint of today, it looks as if Dr. Gibson was at least a year too late. But the notice of the visit, which Dr. Overgaard found in his papers, is proof that the other Ontario universities did not welcome an addition to their number that would affect the amount of government money available for each of them. I wager they didn't envisage the founding of at least four more Ontario universities in the near future (Windsor, Brock, Laurentian—and WLU). To demonstrate that what goes around comes around, this is how the president of the University of Toronto described funding problems in 1996:

The University of Toronto has taken no position on the creation of private universities but insists that if they are created they receive no public funds of any kind. It is abundantly clear that the province has great difficulty meeting the costs of our 17 public universities. As a result it would be the height of folly to permit any further diminution in support for the public universities by extending support to new private institutions. Nor must they be allowed to undermine the value of an Ontario university degree. Current provincial policy permits the full privatization of particular programs—our executive MBA, for example—and the university will seek even greater flexibility to combine public and private funds in creative ways to provide excellent innovative programs. (*University of Toronto Magazine*, 24, no. 2.)

I also offer an excerpt from a report of the advisory panel on future directions for post-secondary education (*Laurier News*, January 28, 1997):

> 18. We recommend that Ontario's policy precluding the establishment of new, privately financed universities be amended to permit, under strict conditions, the establishment of privately financed, not-for-profit universities with the authority to grant degrees with a secular name. Strict conditions and standards must apply to institutional mission and governance structures; institutional and academic quality, as determined by nationally or internationally recognized peer review; financial responsibility; and protection of students in the event of institutional failure. These conditions and standards should be developed by the advisory body on post-secondary education recommended in this report.

These pronouncements prove only that government policy on higher education has not yet lost its ambiguity. It is not surprising that parties with widely diverse aims might all feel that they could gain official support when the authorities are so equivocal.

At one point it seems that the opposition of the other universities to Dr. Hagey's project was so strong that he wrote a letter explaining that the new entity would be under our existing arrangement with Western. This was a surprise to Dr. Hall, the president of UWO who was one of Dr. Hagey's leading opponents, and the author had to go before the relevant body (it may have been the

AUCC) and apologize, which I am told he did with tears—though nothing changed in his planning.

The Lutheran loyalists were aware of the AUCC campaign, and wished it well, but more was needed if Waterloo College was to be saved.

While the plans for the new university were in such a state of confusion, rumour reigned. There were those who just enjoyed carrying news from one Waterloo campus to the other, but there were also double agents. One who had been a respected graduate of the college became some sort of aide to the college president, with access to records, minutes of meetings, etc., while at the same time working for Dr. Hagey. (He as much as admitted it to me. Dr. Overgaard said he also confessed it to him.) People who engaged in conversation about the academic situation in Waterloo, while safely seated in a restaurant far from here, found that news of their opinions got to Dr. Hagey before they did. Punishment for opposition could be dire. I asked why a certain lady was so strong a supporter of Dr. Hagey, and was told that her husband worked for one of the backers of the new university, and his job depended on her loyalty to the new regime.

If this were fiction it could be given a whiff of mystery by mentioning that someone on the loyalist side had a spy camera that could copy documents. I am not saying it was used, but it might have been. (I myself had one later. This was before the era of easy xeroxing, and the little cameras could produce adequate copies for researchers.)

Before going on with the story of academic plans and counterplans, I pause for a moment to answer a hypothetical objection from today. What has all this to do with things that really matter: race, gender, age, sexuality, ethnic/regional identities, physical and mental health (I take the list from an article in the *Laurier News*)? I myself would add the most important at the moment: jobs. Dear reader, I am describing the 1950s. There were no homeless, there were no food banks, people in Waterloo with darker skin (and especially on campus) lived like everyone else. On campus the president of the freshman class was non-white. What we now call gays seemed to live lives as peaceful as they wanted them to be. Wife-beaters were known to the neighbours and looked down on. (One used to live on Albert Street opposite the college. His wife and family used to take refuge with the head of the seminary who occupied the house where the seminary building now stands.)

From the list I borrowed above, only the matter of "ethnic/ regional identities" seems relevant in the attempt to save Waterloo College, and I am not sure how the *bien pensant* would view the determination of a Scandinavian Lutheran to save his religious/ ethnic heritage from being absorbed into a cultural mixture without any particular flavour or idiosyncrasy. At the time it seemed to be important, and I applauded it.

There were many injustices in the society of the 1950s. There was the suffering that comes to anyone in any era—but there were jobs then and the prospect of jobs for following generations. And there was a feeling that the future would be prosperous.

23

My vagueness about chronology includes the date when Dr. Overgaard called me to say that the loyalists were thinking of consulting a lawyer to get advice on preparing a strategy that would seem to follow Dr. Hagey's plans and yet leave room for a declaration of independence. It would be a costly move. I at once offered to contribute what I could, as did all the other loyalists. I think I sent him a cheque.

He had heard Malcolm Robb, of the Supreme Court of Ontario, speaking to a local gathering and had been impressed by his clear thinking. Dr. Overgaard went to our president and asked if he and Dr. Dolbeer, our chaplain, could go as a delegation to visit Mr. Robb. I understand that the lawyer outlined the only possible strategy, which was to continue to participate in the negotiations with Queen's Park for a charter for the new university, but to hold out for a subsidiary charter for a Waterloo Lutheran University, along the line of the charter held by Victoria College in the University of Toronto through which Victoria held control over Emmanuel College, its theological branch. WLU would in the same way have its satellite, the Lutheran Seminary. The only difference would be that Victoria held its charter in abeyance. When WLU had its charter safe and sound, we could declare independence and continue on our own.

Perhaps I was most impressed by the news that Mr. Robb had refused our money. He seems not to have been in favour of Premier Frost's eagerness to found a new Ontario university, and was quite happy to assist in spoiling his plans a bit. Dr. Overgaard asked him to accept five dollars for a cigar. We were, as I have said before, younger and simpler then.

I do not believe that Dr. Delton Glebe, who now was chairman of the Lutheran board, has ever received due credit for his skill as a negotiator while the act to incorporate the new universities (St. Jerome's was also given a charter) was being prepared.

It all worked out as Mr. Robb had advised. When the split came, we still had some connection with the new University of Waterloo through our science courses, which would be given there for a fee. When the price was raised a year or so later, Dean Schaus resolved to start our own science area, and hired a distinguished veteran of administration in the air force, and some others to set it up. As a result we now have—some forty years later—an impressive science building, and a student-centred science curriculum that has produced some serious graduate research scientists, and has contributed general science courses for the rest of the campus.

But we must go back a bit, because before independence came the decisive special meeting of synod on May 12, 1963. The campaigns regarding the fate of Waterloo College seemed to have ended in its dissolution. The Lutheran board had decided to give up the college. Everyone felt things were settled. I recall that during the examination period I entertained as many as possible of my colleagues at lunch, a few at a time after the morning examinations so that those invigilating could come directly to my place from the examination halls. Though I didn't speak it, I was convinced that I would probably never see them again for I would leave the college in the hands of Dr. Hagey, and most of them would probably be part of the new university. I wanted them to recall our association in the college with some pleasure, and even more I wanted them to see the Breithaupt estate, in which I had a tiny flat, because it too was passing away, to be sold for development. (The church group who acquired the estate promptly cut down the trees that had been chosen by the original owners to give examples of all species that could be grown in our area.) Our gatherings were really pleasant. No one referred to the future.

In the background, the loyalist party was attempting to force a special meeting of synod to consider the decision of the Lutheran board to give up the college. Such a mutiny was provided for in the synodical constitution, but it had to be requested by a minimum number of church members. The required number of signatures was obtained, chiefly by the efforts of Dr. Arthur and Dr. Fred Little, but there was some procedural flaw in this first attempt and the whole thing had to be undertaken a second time. The date was set: May 12, and all the parties concerned were mustering their forces.

The meeting was moderated by Dr. Fry from the American Lutheran head office. My impression is that he thought the demand for the meeting was a defiance of authority in that it questioned the decision of the college board. Also, I recalled the meetings I attended in Gettysburg where I heard Lutherans debating the future of their American colleges. One speaker pointed out that, in pioneer days, at least one Lutheran Ladies' Aid went so far as to build a road (which the civic authorities felt could not be done), but that now in more settled times people left matters like education and road-building to the state. The latent problem was, of course, money. Could the private sector go on funding institutions of higher learning? Whatever the reason, the moderator was not at all pleased at the end of the day when the special meeting voted two to one in favour of retaining Waterloo College for the Lutherans. I am told that several eloquent speeches swayed the assembly, speeches which I hope are in the synod archives, though I am told those records are closed.

The decision was made by Lutherans only, but here I want to mention my own unintended contribution. I earlier described in some detail the Lutheran refugees from areas in the hands of the Soviet Union, or to an extent under its domination (as Finland), who now lived in our area. Among them I noted especially my vocal coach (a former leading mezzo in the Estonian state opera) and her husband (an official of the Estonian Ministry of Finance). The struggles that were taking place around me left me with no one to whom I could speak openly about what was going on. Friends off campus could not understand, and besides I didn't want to add to the rumours that by this time were not only spread by word of mouth but were almost every day repeated in the local paper. My Estonian friends were different. They had been no strangers to controversy even in their good times before the war: operas and governments are not run by non-combatants. They were an honorable and sophisticated man and woman of the world, and I was fortunate to be able to share with them week after week my stories of the latest moves in the battle for the college.

They were especially interested in the historian who, you will recall, was the leader of the rebel party, and especially interested in his fondness for the Soviet Union. To them anyone who believed that system was a success was either a subversive agent or what the Irish now spell as an "eejit." They had seen the gap in the standard of living between their own society, and that in Russia, and put that gap into any discussion of ideology. Look at clothing, for instance. When the Russians arrived to take over Estonia, the women hurried to the shops to buy gowns for the forthcoming celebrations. The Estonian guests at the first official reception were almost overcome with laughter when they saw the women resplendent in nightgowns and negligees which, in their ignorance of the language, they had thought were evening gowns.

My coach told the story of one pathetic attempt of a Russian officer to overcome the gap. She saw a group of burly Russian soldiers washing themselves in a public fountain while an officer admonished them to "wash culturally," as she translated it.

When my friends realized that their Lutheran college was going into the hands of people whose leader admired the Russian communist state, they took steps to ensure that the refugee representatives at the special meeting knew that—and I think it had some effect on the vote. I hadn't intended this result—and perhaps my friends weren't the sole influence on the outcome either because many refugees had children attending the college who may have reported on the political ideology of the historian. It is ironic that his assurance as leader of his party may have been its greatest liability.

So the college was to stay in the hands of the Lutherans. Dr. Overgaard did not give me details but said that board members were resigning right and left. I presume they were being replaced, but the whole community, not only the Lutheran party, was in turmoil. The decision was conveyed to the parishioners of Mount Zion Evangelical Church on May 22, 1960 in their weekly notice. (Dr. Glebe, later the head of the college board was the pastor there.) I include some of the contents of the church bulletin to show that the usual life of a Lutheran parish was going to continue even if the sky was falling. The threat in the sky was financial. Where would the church as a whole get the money to support a first-class post-secondary institution—which was the only kind that would be viable? Even allowing for the strength of the 1960 dollar, an offering of $515.97 over the whole synod was not going to go far.

> WATERLOO COLLEGE is in the "headlines" these days. In a 2-1 vote our Canada Synod at a special meeting last Thursday, decided not to federate with the University of Waterloo (the non-church group), unless more acceptable terms are offered by The University. Federation was rejected apparently because Synod felt the University's present terms (1) do not measure up to the articles of agreement between the College and the University enacted by Provincial Legislature March 1959, (2) interfere with the College's Christian emphasis, (3) endanger the College's autonomy and identity. Mr. Reinhardt Schmidt and The Pastor represented Mount Zion at this Special Meeting.

> OFF THE RECORD (Sun. May 15/59)

> | | Offering | Attendance |
> |---|---|---|
> | Current | 147.83 | 151 |
> | Missions | 73.35 | |
> | Building | 274.10 | |
> | Sun. School | 20.69 | 136 |
> | Nursery | | 2 |
> | | 515.97 | |

> (Bulletin, May 22, 1960, Mount Zion
> Evangelical Lutheran Church, Waterloo)

My survey of our financing as an independent body will be deficient in many details, including dates, but I believe it is generally correct.

The federal government had decided to give money to Canadian universities. This was in spite of the constitutional right of provinces to control education. At the time when the list of universities eligible for the grant was published, Waterloo Lutheran University did not yet exist. The link with Western had been broken and the articles giving us a charter had not been signed. We were in limbo. Dr. Overgaard made a point of interviewing all the presidents of the AUCC to ask if they would support us in our request to join the list and, he says, they all agreed. As a result we were added to the fortunate number.

So far so good, *but* the grant had to be matched by the university or the deal was off. A Sunday school collection, though given with a full heart, would not be enough. It was totally impossible to charge tuition fees that would carry the cost of a good university. Wealthy donors there were, but not many of them were Lutheran, and we had not yet anything that would attract money from the corporate sector.

Dr. Overgaard wondered if a federal arrangement for financial help with housing could be extended to university residences. I understand that one could borrow money for housing with loans at favourable rates which would be backed by the government of Canada.

At least we know that WLU was able to get the housing loan, which he then advised the board to use as the matching money for the federal grant. The scheme worked, and Dr. Overgaard advised his friends at other newly independent institutions to get in on it quickly because he was sure the loophole would be closed as soon as discovered by tardy officialdom—as it was. In the meantime we and our friends had acquired buildings that would be assets to use in further funding schemes. We were on our way.

24

Wʜᴇɴ I ᴛʀʏ ᴛᴏ ʀᴇᴄᴀʟʟ ᴛʜᴇ ᴀꜰᴛᴇʀᴍᴀᴛʜ of the decision to make Waterloo College an independent university, I cannot sort out events. Dr. Axford, the president, resigned in 1961, but the search for a new president must have begun before this time. I recall that an official from the American synod arrived to help in the transition; I was delighted to hear that he was a von Maltke. It seemed to put our affairs in the big league—a very big league indeed. I made an excuse to get to the administration offices to see the man I supposed to be a family connection of the great general. We didn't at the time know much about the German opponents of Hitler, but if we had it would have been a further reason to get at least a glimpse of one of the family. He proved to be a helpful man of medium height and unassuming manner. I don't think that he equated our problems in Waterloo with the family's campaigns against France—or against Hitler, but for me there was a reminder that the world was bigger than Waterloo County. It was very important to retain some perspective as the reaction to our decision became more and more distressing.

The newspapers had reported the news of the new university with disapproval, but the most damaging account was in a Toronto paper. It was an article on an inner page with a byline, stating that the new institution had no hope of succeeding, partly because it would lose most of its faculty and those who remained were incompetent. I recall little of the text because I deliberately put it out of my mind, but my friends at Western interpreted one line as a direct attack on *my* credentials, so much so that Dr. Klinck who had once been Dean of Waterloo College wanted me to sue the paper. I heard that the editor had not read the article before publication, and that when he did he talked to a legal advisor about the possibility of a suit for damages. I know that any further publicity would harm no one more than me and would hinder Waterloo Lutheran University in the next campaign for academic respectability. I speculated about the author. Was he a friend of the historian who might well wish us to suffer from his defection and that of his friends? Was he paid by Dr. Hagey and the new University of Waterloo? We didn't bother to try to find out.

Locally we had plenty to do in fending off attacks. It seemed that whenever I went to a social gathering, I was met with angry questions. "Why didn't you join them?" said a group of medical men at a party given by one of our graduates. I could hardly say that, speaking for myself, I wasn't wanted, and had never been asked to join.

Someone asked me recently if the possibility of forming a Lutheran college in the new arrangement was ever considered. I don't recall any discussion of that kind. I rather think that relations had become so strained that any close connection with Dr. Hagey and friends would be impossible.

Earlier in this narrative I gave my impressions of the differences that were underneath the apparent tranquility of life in Kitchener and Waterloo, so I shall not repeat them here except to remark that I think that the acrimony that developed around the academic situation came to a degree from a resurfacing of the old enmities in the community: Germans versus "Canadians," Lutherans versus other denominations. Once again a foreign group had refused to be one with the rest of the community. I sensed a feeling of rejection— almost of being jilted, that lasted a long time. Some years after the split, one of our Spanish professors and his wife invited me to a house party that would include members of the faculty of Romance Languages from the University of Waterloo. I found myself situated for the evening on a sofa beside a French-Canadian lady who berated me about our standing apart, "You should have been *forced* to join us. The province shouldn't have allowed it" was what I heard all evening. I couldn't understand the feeling in her voice—I still can't.

What really mattered was the reaction of students and potential faculty. I don't think we ever contemplated giving up, but when pre-registration showed that we would have enough students to be viable we probably all relaxed a bit. Most of our former students returned, though a number of them had launched a campaign of their own to keep the original Waterloo College as the centre of the new university (but, I suspect, without the religious connection). One of the campaigners with whom I am in touch, is very cagey on that point.

Would we get the necessary faculty? As I have said, some of the anti-Lutheran party remained, if reluctantly, and there were others who were willing to risk their academic reputations by joining us. Dr. Overgaard has reminded me that our personal reputations at other universities probably helped us. In English we had applications from a member of the Extension faculty at Toronto who was an old friend of mine. We were also fortunate in hiring a young woman, just returned from studies at Cambridge, who had been offered a position in a western university but wanted to remain in Ontario not too far from her recently widowed mother. Other departments were filling up their quotas of teaching staff as well.

A very serious crisis came out of the blue. In those days, the Ontario College of Education ran summer courses for honours graduates so that they could go immediately into the schools after one summer and obtain their further credentials in the holidays. Dean Schaus learned that a number of our honours students had been informed officially that graduates of Waterloo Lutheran University would not be eligible for entrance to the College of Education. Since most of our honours students in arts were planning to teach, this would force them to transfer to another university if they wanted to work in Ontario. (Would colleges of education in other provinces have accepted them? We didn't try to find out.) Dean Schaus immediately called the head of the Ontario college and asked for an appointment, and he and I set out for Toronto. We didn't plan any strategy on the way, but waited to see how we were received. I recall that the dean had a courteous exchange with a policeman who pointed out that he should have stopped at a pedestrian crossing. His mind hadn't been on his driving.

I have never been able to understand the situation. We were received very pleasantly. I reminded the head that the student who had recently been named the best in practice teaching was one of our graduates, and that the others we had sent to him had done very well. He smiled amiably as he recalled them. Why then would he bar our future students? We really didn't get any answer, but we left knowing that the ban would not take effect.

Later we heard a rumour that the head was a brother-in-law of Premier Frost who had been so determined in his championship of the University of Waterloo. Had he been forced by family pressure to put an obstacle in our way because we had refused to be destroyed by the new arrangement? Later the Roman Catholic nephew of the same head came to us as an English honours student, and did very well—and enjoyed himself. It still is a mystery to me.

This might be the time to ask why Premier Frost was 1) so bent upon putting an end to Roman Catholic and Lutheran academic entities in Ontario and 2) so much a supporter of the University of Waterloo. Didn't Dr. Overgaard tell me that Frost gave the University of Waterloo as much for one new building as he gave to all the rest of the universities in Ontario that year? At meetings of the learned societies in those years, people used to come up and whisper in my ear, "What has Hagey got on Frost?" a natural enough query, but I never knew the answer. Later the son of the next premier became one of our graduates. The Ontario government seemed to have forgiven us. Indeed, we heard that we were used as an example of academic frugality when other Ontario universities pleaded poverty. But that was when our grants were coming from the federal government. When the provinces got control of that fund, our share was cut in half. The pressure was again put on a church-related university.

In the meantime, provincial funding was extended to cover Roman Catholic high schools. One should not look for consistency in political decisions. Perhaps Premier Davis might have later extended full grants to each Ontario university regardless of church connections. Today there doesn't seem to be much enthusiasm for church-related universities unless they are self-supporting and offer no financial problem to the Ontario government.

There is a legend that Simon Fraser University was founded because the government wanted an institution that it could influence. The older University of British Columbia cherished its independence; the new one might be more amenable. In Ontario, Premier Frost may have been frustrated by the intransigence of the established universities and wanted one that he could mould more closely to what he thought the province needed for the future.

I recall that the English departments of Toronto, Queen's, and Western were asked to institute alternative honours programmes that would be easier than the regular ones. There was a push to have all teachers in Ontario secondary schools fully qualified, which meant graduation with an honours degree. There were many in the system who found it impossible to meet that standard: I knew one man who had tried to upgrade in Toronto and failed each time. In a way, the intention may have been to force the less able teachers out of the schools, but there was sure to be a political reaction as voters who lost their jobs, along with their families and friends, became angry with those who were trying to improve standards.

The meeting of representatives of the English departments was held in Toronto. (Was it in the Cloisters? I seem to recall that the setting was familiar.) The head at Western had included me as part of their system, and there were some others who were not heads of independent universities. We all spoke against any watering-down of requirements for the honours degree, and Professor Woodhouse was directed to inform the government of our decision.

After the new University of Waterloo was in existence and its courses were running, I believe some arrangement was made for summer school courses that the ministry would regard as at honours level. I don't think there was a general awareness of what was happening, and one hopes that some poor souls were able to finish their careers in high school teaching with something that resembled honours standing.

Later the Ministry for Universities became concerned about the great need for faculty in the new universities, and suggested that instead of confining all graduate students to the PhD as the final degree, some could be shifted into a master's programme which would make them eligible for university postings. Here the University of Waterloo was not alone in acceding to official suggestions (and a number of graduates from the less rigorous course came on the market.) The problem was to persuade universities to hire them. It was still clear that the PhD was more prestigious, and institutions like ours, trying to gain academic respectability, could not afford to hire people with the MPhil who would expect to have tenure, and would not be too happy if they could not advance through the ranks to finally become full professors. To go back and enter a PhD programme was not easy, and who would bother if a job was guaranteed without it?

I was not pleased to note that a number of the MPhil candidates were women. I had the unhappy duty of refusing to hire a couple of faculty wives from the University of Waterloo who had taken the MPhil in the hope that we would not be as demanding as would a larger university. I did hire one MPhil graduate from the University of Toronto but on a fixed-term contract, which we terminated when it ran out, with the recommendation that she go on to get the PhD if she wanted us to give her any further consideration. I heard that she gave the University of Toronto a few bad moments by declaring that they had given her the MPhil under false pretences, and I heard too that when York balked at her credentials she joined an especially effective feminist group who managed to overcome York's objections.

I have been circuitous about this but I can now admit that I believe a concession to candidates for academic employment when they have not the time, or the endurance—or may we say the ability—to go further, throws a shadow over those who take advantage of its faculty members.

To conclude this story of Waterloo College, I do not recall that there was any kind of celebration marking its ending and the birth of the new Waterloo Lutheran University. We knew that all our creativity and energy and hard work would be needed if we were to be regarded by the general public as well as by the academic establishment as anything but a satellite of the new University of Waterloo.

We did succeed in building a university in the physical sense as well as academically, and, less obviously, in spirit. But that is another story.